Sweet Tea, Fried Chicken, & Lazy Dogs

reflections on north carolina life

SWEET TEA,
FRIED CHICKEN,
AND LAZY DOGS

reflections on north carolina life

∽

Bill Thompson

Our State
NORTH CAROLINA
BOOKS

published by Mann Media Inc.
Greensboro, North Carolina

Publisher: Bernard Mann
Editor and Associate Publisher: Mary Best
Cover Illustrator: Eric Westbrook
Cover Designer: Larry Williams
Marketing Director: Amy Jo Wood
Production Director: Cheryl Bissett
Distribution Manager: Erica Derr

Library of Congress Cataloging-in-Publication Data

Thompson, Bill, 1943, Sept. 18-
Sweet tea, fried chicken, and lazy dogs : reflections on North
Carolina life / Bill Thompson.
p. cm.
ISBN 0-9723396-1-2 (alk. paper)
1. North Carolina--Social life and customs--Anecdotes. 2. Country
life--North Carolina--Anecdotes. 3. North
Carolina--Biography--Anecdotes. 4. Thompson, Bill, 1943, Sept.
18---Anecdotes. I. Title.
F254.6.T48 2003
975.6'043--dc21
2003013481

∾

For Bill and Mildred

my parents

∾

TABLE OF CONTENTS

～

Chapter One: Country Creatures

❦

Chapter Two: Hearth and Home

✃

Chapter Three: Tar Heel Travels

❧

Chapter Four: Real Characters

↩

Chapter Five: Southern Ways

∾

Chapter Six: Music of Life

෫෬

Chapter Seven: Rhythm of the Seasons

❀

Chapter Eight: Just a Thought

∾

Chapter Nine: The Wonderful World of Fiction

Acknowledgments

I t is a temptation to call this book a culmination of an effort. It is, however, more accurate to call it one more step in my education that has led to this point. To give proper credit to all those who have contributed to what follows between these pages would mean going all the way back to my teachers in high school and college. I would have to acknowledge all those writers whose books about North Carolina and the rest of the South I absorbed and assimilated. I would have to thank all those folks who have told me stories through the years: those who came into my family's store, the folks who came up to me at various functions across the state to tell me a story because they could identify with the ones I had told them. So, I do thank them.

There are some particular individuals who may not have considered themselves teachers but who taught me nevertheless. Thom Billington was an editor at *The News Reporter* in Whiteville when I was working in television. I began to get ideas for stories that did not necessarily lend themselves to the more visual medium of television. Thom allowed me to turn those ideas into a column for that paper, and that eventually led to writing for other newspapers. Thom was not one to pass out compliments easily, but he once told someone that I wrote "an above average column." That praise encouraged me to continue.

Jim and Les High, also of *The News Reporter*, encouraged me and promoted my column to other papers. Having to meet a regular deadline essentially created a forced discipline, which made me write even when the muse eluded me.

Then, one day, I asked Arlene Gutterman, a sales representative for *Our State* magazine, to give some copies of my work to Mary Best, who was the editor of the increasingly popular magazine. In 2001, when Mary and senior editor Elizabeth Hudson told me they would like to feature my writing in each monthly issue of the magazine, I was flattered. They encouraged me and gave me exposure to folks who seemed really to like what I wrote. When publisher Bernie Mann would write little notes of encouragement on the checks from the magazine, I took that as a real compliment. And Amy Jo Wood asked me to be a part of The Best of Our State at The Grove Park Inn in Asheville.

Fortunately, Mary took charge of the new book-publishing arm of *Our State* and agreed to oversee the development of this book. I'm sure I have tested her patience.

For all these people, I am especially grateful.

So, here it is, folks. I hope you're proud of what I have done. I am.

— *Bill Thompson*

Preface

Why did I want to write a book? Apart from the monetary consider-ations, I figured writing a book, this particular kind of book, would be a way of saying something about what made me who I am. I hope this will discourage any further derogatory designations that I am a "self-made" anything. I don't intend for this to be an autobiography, although there is much of my own life in the stories.

One appellation that is frequently applied to males in my part of the country is "good ol' boy." This is a compliment. Despite the outcry from folks who have a misconception about good ol' boys, such a designation simply means such a person is a good friend who doesn't care much for some of the constrictions of "polite society." Despite the fact that I have had the opportunity to get a good education, travel extensively, and meet all kinds of people and experience a wide spectrum of activities, I am still, in my mind, a "good ol' boy."

I am a product of North Carolina, specifically a small, rural com-munity called Hallsboro. The people I have known here have been ordinary people who happen to possess the distinctive characteristics of other people who have lived in similar environments. That in itself does not make them unusual. In fact, it is that commonality that con-nects them with people everywhere. Those common experiences have shaped me.

John Donne insightfully wrote that "No man is an island, entire of itself; every man is a piece of the continent, a part of the main ..." So, by inference, I am a part of everyone who might read this book and, by extension, they are a part of me.

I have been fortunate to be able to look at my home from the perspective of someone who has left it for a time and returned. Sometimes when we are so close to people and things, we can't appreciate what is there. We have to back off to see how really rare and important they are.

I don't want to imply that this compilation of stories and essays is of earth-shaking importance. It's not. It's not going to have a major effect on anybody. At the same time, when I was listening to all those folks who came into my family's country store there in Hallsboro, I never imagined I would be using those stories as references for this book. So, these are not so much my stories as they are the stories of all those people I have met.

This is a collection of essays and short stories. By definition an essay is an opinion based on a personal point of view. What follows are my opinions about a wide variety of things, all of which reflect my exposure not only to Hallsboro but also the rest of the world.

I hope in this book to show my appreciation for all those folks who have become a part of me. I hope all those people who have never heard of Hallsboro or me can appreciate that which has made us both unique. Some stories will make you laugh, some will make you cry, and some will make you think. And some may make you wonder what in the world is on my mind.

But I hope you will enjoy them.

— *Bill Thompson*

Sweet Tea, Fried Chicken, & Lazy Dogs

reflections on north carolina life

~ ~ ~

CHAPTER ONE

country creatures

~ ~ ~

In Defense of Chickens

From time to time I am compelled to defend chickens. Far too many people look down on chickens as the lowliest element in the barnyard. Such is not the case.

Columbus brought chickens to America in 1493. Why they didn't come with the first load in 1492, I don't know. In any case, Columbus must have appreciated them because he had only so much room on those little ships, and he could only bring the most important animals with him.

Chickens make an important contribution to the American diet by producing eggs. They make an even more significant personal commitment by becoming the chief element in what is often called the finest food ever created: fried chicken.

Southern fried chicken is probably the single most popular and universally consumed food ever to come from this region of the country. (Although not universally consumed or popular outside of a small section of the South, boiled peanuts are not included here since that delicacy is not usually served as an entrée.) Not counting Colonel Sanders' recipe (which isn't fried anyway), the basic method of cooking fried chicken hasn't changed much through the years. You just cut up the pieces of chicken, cover them in flour, and fry them in hot fat.

Remember, that is just the basics. Every Southern cook has their own variation that they swear is not only the best but is the original "Southern fried" as well. (Since Columbus left no recipe for fried chicken, we have to assume he was not the originator of that particular culinary art.)

The recipes vary widely. Some folks fry chicken in lard, some prefer vegetable oil, some others pan-fry, and others deep-fat-fry. Some add cornmeal or milk or eggs. Some season with salt and pepper, while others add hot sauce, garlic, or lemon.

About the only aspect of Southern fried chicken that few debate is the best way to eat it: with your fingers. I say almost the only way because there are a few great Southern ladies who have developed the art of skinning a chicken bone with a knife and fork and insist that any other way is "tacky, tacky, tacky." It is a unique and educational experience to watch someone eat fried chicken with knife and fork. Like watching a surgeon at work.

Because of the popularity of fried chicken, a boom in fast-food chicken places has caused a tremendous increase in the demand for chickens. The result is a low-quality chicken compared to the kind originally cast into the frying pan by our ancestors. There can be no comparison between a chicken raised in a small cage where its only exercise is eating the piles of food placed before it and the spunky chicken who had to scratch the ground for the scattered remnants of cracked corn tossed to it. The weak meat of the caged chicken lacks the flavor of the chicken who survived because of sheer "cluck."

So I defend the lowly chicken. Think what the tables of so many Southern families would have missed if Columbus had decided to leave the chickens back in Spain. Think about how many Sunday dinners would have just been another serving of ham and potato salad.

What if Columbus had decided to bring pizza instead?

The Great Escape

As I drive along the back roads of North Carolina, I see hundreds of hog houses. These oft-maligned pork factories don't appear to belong to pig farmers, at least any of the pig farmers I have known. They are much too mechanized and automated to be compared to the hog operations that were the common method of raising hogs just a few years ago.

Back in the 1960s, J.L. Stanley worked for the Boys Home of North Carolina at Lake Waccamaw. The home raised its own pork in an open-air pen much like those that had been used for centuries. The pen was located on a hill some distance from a swamp, which abuts the canal that wraps around a portion of the lake.

The boys in residence helped raise the hogs. For various periods of time, they were assigned to work with J.L., primarily helping with the task of feeding them. J.L. was a good teacher and a tolerant supervisor — he had to be to get work out of the boys, who were not particularly interested in raising hogs.

On a hot Saturday afternoon in August, all of the 20 or so hogs being kept in that pen escaped into the swamp. When the escape was discovered, J.L. was promptly called to find the hogs and return them to the pen.

On any given Saturday afternoon in the summer, it was difficult to find a boy on the campus. The cool waters of the lake beckoned, some of the guys had arranged to meet some of the local girls at the skating rink, and some had gone to Whiteville to the movies.

Only some poor soul who had been "campused" as punishment for some misconduct was likely to be found to assist J.L. in recovering the hogs. Alvin was the only one available.

When approached by J.L. to assist in the recovery, Alvin was certainly more than reluctant to leave the air-conditioned residence and go out in the humid heat to find hogs. But J.L. prevailed, and Alvin was instructed to stand in the fenced road just down from the gate going into the pen. J.L. was to go down into the swamp, find the hogs, and drive them toward Alvin, who would turn them back into the pen.

It was mid-afternoon and the temperature was near 90 degrees with the typical swamp humidity undisturbed by even the smallest breeze. Alvin dutifully stood in the road, the sun beating down on him, as J.L. searched the swamp for the hogs. An hour went by, then two, and Alvin's commitment to the task waned considerably. Still, J.L. and the hogs did not appear.

After waiting for what seemed to Alvin plenty of time for the hog roundup to be completed, he returned to the coolness of the residence, lay down on the cool floor of the kitchen, and eventually fell asleep.

Of course, Alvin's absence was unknown to J.L. as he struggled through the heat, the swamp mud, and knee-deep water; bruised his shins on cypress stumps; and watched for snakes and alligators as he urged his recalcitrant swine back to their lodging.

As J.L. topped the hill leading back to the hog pen, he got the hogs into a run, hoping they wouldn't try to circle around him. It wasn't until he had them in the fenced road that he saw that Alvin wasn't there.

Hogs ran helter-skelter onto the campus, down to the lakefront, across the street to the town hall and fire station, and slowed down only when they reached the gardens of some of the Lake Waccamaw residents. All while Alvin slept.

With the help of townspeople and anybody else he could find, J.L. got the hogs back in the pen. Then he went looking for Alvin.

There is no need to go into detail on what transpired between J.L. and Alvin. Suffice it to say that Alvin's restriction to the campus was continued for a very long time.

I thought about J.L. and Alvin as I drove by the new hog operations. I'll bet the folks who operate those modern facilities have somebody just like Alvin working for them. The business may change, but people don't.

The Carolina Yard Dog

I stopped at a service station down in Brunswick County the other day to get a Pepsi and a pack of Nabs. In the course of my respite from driving, I met a most unusual man.

He drove up to put some air in the tires of his old blue Chevrolet pickup truck. I don't know what model or year the truck was, but it had seen a lot of dirt-road miles. Grime covered the truck from one end to the other, and someone had finger-written "bound for glory" on the passenger side of the cab.

The driver was much like the truck: covered with dirt and the victim of a lot of miles. His reddish-gray beard covered most of his face, but I could still see the creases around his eyes. Those eyes didn't fit the rest of the man. They seemed to sparkle, and the lines around his eyes must have fought their way through his beard and on down to that grin that showed several teeth missing. Altogether, he presented a sort of amiable, if disheveled, appearance.

But it wasn't the man who got my interest so much as it was the dog he had chained in the back of his truck. No dog box for that canine; only a big chain attached to the collar and passed through the center of a spare tire held him in the truck. He didn't look like he needed any restraint. He was resting peacefully, stretched out with his head looking toward the stranger who peeked over the side.

He didn't look like any particular breed, although I thought it was a hound of some kind. "Nice dog you got there. What kind is it?" I asked.

"That, my friend, is a hundred percent purebred Carolina Yard Dog," the man replied. "Raised him from a pup. His mama and his daddy was both champion Yard Dogs."

"I don't believe I've ever seen or heard of a purebred Yard Dog before," I said.

"Well, they are pretty rare, but my family has been breeding them for generations. We practice some real selective breeding. Keep only the best for ourselves, and we're right particular about who we sell the rest of them to. Can't just no ordinary person treat a Carolina Yard Dog like he's got to be treated."

"What makes them so special?" I asked.

"The main thing we look for is a good temperament. A good Yard Dog has got to take things slow and easy. We can't have no dog that's too energetic. We don't want him to go no faster than a walk, and he can't cover more than about a hundred feet without resting. A hundred feet is about the distance of our yard there to the house. That's how we come up with the name, you know.

"The next-best trait we look for is easy keeping. Our dogs don't need worming nor any kind of shots. And, above all, they are not the least bit particular about what they eat, and they don't eat much anyhow. A good Yard Dog is definitely a low-maintenance animal."

"What does this kind of dog do? Does he hunt?" I asked.

"Lord, no! Why, a turtle'd outrun him. A good Yard Dog is the best watchdog you can find. He don't appear vicious, though. In fact, when a stranger comes up in the yard, that dog will just look at him and stare him down. It will usually make an intruder so worried about what the dog is going to do, that the mystery of it will make the stranger leave rather than take a chance on what the dog might do."

"These must be very rare dogs. How many are there?" I asked.

"Very, very few," he replied. "They are so slow and calm it's hard to get them to breed."

Then the man just laughed good and hard and got in his dirty truck and drove away.

The Carolina Yard Cat

Since I have written down my observations regarding the fabled but rare Carolina Yard Dog, my wife pointed out to me that I had, as often occurs, neglected to note the presence of our own Yard Cat. I began to point out to her that I had not really neglected to note the flighty feline who has outlined her domain under our house.

First of all, she isn't our cat. She isn't anybody's cat. She is the offspring of other cats who have lived on the premises without being owned by anybody. As a matter of fact, no human has ever touched this cat, her ancestors, or her descendants. We feed them all, so they stayed for a period of time — and now she stays. I use the term "stays" as most Southerners do instead of "resides" because she has no specific residence. She stays anywhere she wants to stay.

Further proof that she doesn't belong to anybody is the fact that she doesn't even have a name. I had thought of calling her "Miss Kitty" because I just thought that would be so clever. After some reflection, however, I decided not to name her. Having a name denotes some connection between the individual bestowing the name and the individual receiving the name. This cat and I have no relationship on which we could base such titling. In addition, the purpose of having a name is so a person, or cat, can be called to respond in some way to another. It would be a complete waste of time to try to call this cat in expectation of a response.

I should make it clear that I have tried in the past to establish a relationship with this cat. In fact, it took me a while to determine that this cat was, indeed, a female. Even when she was a kitten, she wanted nothing to do with humans. We fed her, made a special little bed for her on the back porch, sat quietly watching her hoping that her curiosity would make her come to us. All to no avail. Not knowing her actual gender, I had thought of naming her "Rhett Butler" because she frankly "didn't give a darn." But, again, I saw the futility of the process.

This cat is in no way a house cat. On those very rare occasions when she has furtively entered the house, she has exited the premises as soon as she was discovered. Her daily habits are not conducive to living in a house. She is accustomed to fairly frequent and violent confrontations with opossums, who stealthily approach her food, which we place on the porch. The fury and violence exhibited by this cat on such occasions would frighten the hungriest intruder. One of the great pictures of nature is the sight of an opossum moving hastily across the lawn with a screaming and clawing cat attached to its back. She is definitely not a house cat.

I have heard people speak of "the morals of an alley cat." Let me assure you that this cat would make an alley cat appear celibate. In the short time she has stayed at our house, she has had several litters of kittens. The fathers are unknown, but judging from the frequency of visits by tomcats, she does not spurn any applicant for paternity.

In at least one respect, my wife is right. This is a Yard Cat. So if I paid homage to the Yard Dog, this is my homage — such as it is — to the Yard Cat.

The Milk Cow Incident

A lmost every day somebody confronts me about the proliferation of incidents of inhumane treatment of animals. Right away, I'm sure you are thinking, "Why him?" The question of why I am sought out as a sounding board for those folks who think that cats are too often put upon, dogs shouldn't be treated like dogs, and that farm animals have rights, too, is one that faces me each day.

I no longer own a dog. The cats that hang around my house do so only because my wife feeds them. The only other animals I come in contact with are horses and a few cows. None of those associations should make me have more than an ordinary understanding of animals and certainly doesn't give me any great insight into how to influence the way people treat animals.

Therefore, I must conclude that the knowledge of an experience with a certain cow of my childhood has leaked out.

One of those summers I spent on my grandmother's farm in Chadbourn is remembered for posterity as the Summer of the Milk Cow Incident. I don't know that it is actually recorded that way in any book, but that's the file name in my memory bank.

I was only about six years old at the time, and everything that happened on a farm was exciting and of tremendous interest to me. Frank, an uncle who was only a few years older than I was, was my teacher. He introduced me to all the wonders the farm held. They were not necessarily wonders to him because he had always been around them and took them for granted. But I saw and questioned everything. I wondered about things such as the ability of chickens to swim, if hogs knew they smelled bad, and, of course, where did all the baby animals come from. In the course of time Frank provided the answers as best he could. (I don't think we ever settled the question of whether hogs knew how they smelled.)

One of my main concerns was exactly what was the usefulness of a milk cow. I saw Frank milk the cow. I drank the milk and wondered if that was all a milk cow did. Surely, to my mind, a milk cow had to do some kind of work to justify her existence. Providing milk didn't require any labor on the part of the cow. Frank did all the work.

I saw the other animals earning their keep. The mules pulled all kinds of equipment. The other animals, including the pigs and chickens, made the ultimate sacrifice in providing food for the table.

So it occurred to me that I should find a way to make the cow do more to justify her existence. I rationalized that any animal as big as a cow (to a six-year-old boy, a cow is very big) should be able to do work similar to a mule, a horse, and similar sized animals. So I took it on myself to teach the milk cow to pull a sled.

By attaching a series of cotton ropes around the cow's neck and to a wooden sled placed directly behind her and then getting her to pull it, I figured I could easily teach the cow something useful.

Boy, was I wrong. When I took hold of the milk cow's halter to move her forward with all that attachment, she took off bellowing and kicking at the ropes and sled. She ran right through a barbed-wire fence and down the dirt road. Frank retrieved her later that day; Grandmama used the then-revered corporal punishment on my person; and a few days later the cow gave milk again.

Surely, this must be the basis for the credibility given me as a consultant on animal abuse. And those seeking advice may be right in at least one aspect. I believe I can explain, based on my experience with that old milk cow, the possible origin of mad cow disease since that was one really mad cow.

♥ ♥ ♥

CHAPTER TWO

hearth and home

♥ ♥ ♥

A New Day for Dads

Almost every day something happens that makes me feel like I am standing still while the world zips on by me. Just last week I stopped at a McDonald's for a midday repast and went into the men's room prior to standing in line with 26 other people to order my meal. There, I saw a sign that was proof I am now way past the mid-century mark and way behind the social curve. The sign said, "This table is provided for changing baby's diapers."

Who would have ever thought such a provision would be necessary in a men's room? When my children were at the stage when such a device was necessary, I made every effort never to need it. I don't mean just in the men's room, I mean never at any time. Changing diapers was something I tried to avoid at all costs.

On those occasions when one of my children was left in my solitary care, I have been known to call a neighbor or put the child's soaked and soiled little body in the car and drive several miles to the home of some soul who would chastise me and then change the diapers.

Their mother could never understand how I could clean out horse stalls with no compunction but would shun changing the diapers of my flesh and blood.

I don't understand it myself, but I know it's not the same thing.

It wasn't that I was insensitive to having my children even momentarily uncomfortable. The fact of the matter was: As soon as I became aware of their condition, I would almost panic to remedy the situation. And I must admit that there were some very rare occasions when I did change their diapers. It may have been because I had misplaced the car keys or the neighbors ignored my calls. I always prided myself on the deft way I connected the Pampers, although it usually had to be done again when their mother returned.

I know this confession must make me sound completely out of step with the modern world, but I was one of those fathers who was not allowed in the delivery room, much less asked to assist with the delivery of the child. I remember the rush to the hospital, the waiting, the anxiety of wondering how everything was going, and the relief and exultation of learning that everybody was okay.

Over the years, as my children were growing up, I often washed them, mended their childhood wounds, consoled them, bragged on them, reprimanded them, encouraged them, cheered them, dressed them, fed them, read to them, and played with them, but the number of times I changed their diapers can be counted on one hand. But I don't think they have suffered unduly because of my omission.

That sign I saw in McDonald's that day is the only such sign I have seen. I'm sure there will be more and more diaper-changing tables available as the role of the father continues to evolve in today's society. It's not a bad evolution. I'm sure that those modern dads who get more involved with the rearing of their children will benefit from the resulting closeness of the relationship. I'm sure the mothers will appreciate it, too. And I'm sure there are some single dads who will relish the opportunity to expand the traditional paternal role. In fact, probably only good can come from the change. About the only negative I can think of is that because of the proliferation of disposable diapers, there may be more clogged-up toilets in the men's rooms.

Mr. Fix It

I have never been known for my mechanical expertise. Anybody who believes that the ability to understand mechanics and fix things is an inherited trait doesn't know me. My father has always been able to fix things. You would think after all those years of watching him repair everything that had a screw or a bolt I would have learned something. Well, I did learn something. I learned it was a lot easier to watch him fix it than it was for me to go to all the trouble myself.

I was reminded of my deficiency in this area when I went out to get in the car to go to work the other morning and realized the ice on the windshield had frozen the wiper blades to the glass. So I figured all I had to do was pull the blades off the ice, turn the wipers on, and everything would be okay. That's not the way it works.

In trying to extricate the wiper blades from the frozen windshield, I found that the ice was stronger than the rubber thingamajig that actually wipes the water from the windshield. So in my haste to make the wipers operable, I detached the thingamajig from the arm of the wiper. Of course, then that piece of rubber was stuck to the glass.

I went inside the house, got a glass of water, and threw the water on the windshield. The blade was still stuck, but the frost of the ice had melted, making it look like I could probably see well enough to drive the car. That appearance was deceptive.

When I got in the car, I turned on the defroster, which immediately caused a fog to cover the window. I wiped off a spot with my hand, thinking that would solve all my problems.

I also realized another principle of physics. If you have a glazed-over windshield facing east in the morning, the light shining on that icy surface will create a glare that would blind a welder.

The defroster was taking an inordinate amount of time melting the ice on the windshield. It occurred to me that since the water I had previously thrown had melted the ice once, I could speed up the melting process considerably by putting water on the remaining icy covering. I pushed the button that squirts water on the windshield, and sure enough that water had not frozen. It didn't, however, clear up anything. In fact, it just gave another layer of glaze to the already blinding covering.

To complicate things, the rubber thingamajig was still not attached to the wiper arm; so when the arm began to move across the windshield, it made a scraping sound closely resembling a fingernail on a blackboard. It didn't remove the glaze at all, but it did knock the rubber thingamajig loose, so I reattached it to the wiper arm. But the ice didn't sweep away.

Then I discovered that if I kept squirting the water on the windshield while the blade was working, I could clear a spot big enough to see through. So I began to drive the car down the driveway and out to the highway. Things were looking pretty good. If I rolled down all the windows I could see fine on both sides, but I realized that trying to drive down the highway in that condition was too dangerous.

That's when I took advantage of my past experience and called my father and asked for advice. He said, "Use the ice scraper in the glove compartment."

He has always had a better knowledge of mechanics than I do.

It's a Liver-and-Onions Night

Tonight, my wife cooked liver and onions for supper. Now I know you probably think that is not exactly the kind of meal you would have chosen if you had a choice. Well, I didn't have a choice, but I would have chosen it anyway.

You see, liver and onions is one of those meals now referred to as "comfort food." In all honesty, it may not be comfort food to everybody, but to me it is.

Comfort food is supposed to go beyond meeting any nutritional needs. It is supposed to make you feel better about yourself, less tense, and more tolerant of your fellow man. Of course, you could get the same feeling if you got a good shot of Demerol, but somehow it just wouldn't be the same.

One reason I like liver and onions is because the smell of liver and onions cooking reminds me of my mother's kitchen when I was growing up. There is a certain feeling you can only find in your mother's kitchen, and that feeling isn't restricted to childhood. When you were in that kitchen, you felt safe, secure, and cared for. It didn't matter if you had experienced a bad day at school or if your best friend had abandoned you; once you were ensconced in Mama's kitchen, all the troubles of the world were washed away.

There used to be a little café on the courthouse square in Whiteville that served liver and onions every Wednesday. I ate there almost every Wednesday I was in town. The café was nothing like Mama's kitchen, but it did seem that for the little time I spent eating lunch there, I was somehow transported back about 40 years. I'll bet a lot of the other folks who were there eating liver and onions felt the same way.

Some people might try to tell me that liver and onions are comparable to hot dogs. Some people think hot dogs are comfort food. That may be. Different food appeals to different people for different reasons. But one reason liver and wieners are similar is that I don't really want to know where they come from. Just let me revel in my ignorance and enjoy my reverie.

Although it is the taste of liver and onions that attracts most folks (who are *attracted* at all), it is the smell of that dish cooking that really attracts me. Particularly in winter or late fall when I would be playing outside just before dark, the smell of liver and onions cooking would signal me to stop whatever I was doing and go home. I had no trouble detecting the smell from some distance since that distinctive smell, like a good wine, seems to travel well.

I must admit that my desire — nay, my appreciation — for liver and onions is not shared by everyone. I cannot remember any of my friends inviting themselves over to my house for liver and onions. In my travels I have not found liver and onions on many menus in some of the finer restaurants. That is one reason I often frequent the local restaurants when I visit other towns. You can find liver-and-onions restaurants much like you find good barbecue joints — by the smell.

Sometimes when the weight of the world seems too heavy for me to bear, when the stress of making one more decision is one too many, when the sound of the telephone assaults my ears like fingernails on a blackboard, I seek out liver and onions.

Oh, yes. One other attraction that liver and onions has for the harried life: It is almost always eaten alone.

Cleanliness Isn't Next to Me

Sometimes I think things are too clean. Not that I'm in favor of filth or germs, it's just that I'd like for things to be less antiseptic and a little more earthy, a little more personal.

I know that when my wife reads this she will think this is a rationalization for my untidy lifestyle. She is obsessive about cleanliness and views my less intensive efforts at dirt removal as a direct affront to her attempt to keep our humble abode spotless.

Once I jokingly told some friends that our house was so clean we could eat off the floor — if it weren't so uncomfortable. That attempt at humor was lost on her. She said she was considering serving meals in the Asian manner where we could all stretch out on little pallets placed around a table six inches off the floor.

She is not alone in her quest for perfect cleanliness. I'm sure all of us at some time or other have eaten meals at people's homes where the hostess began removing and washing the glasses and silverware before we finished eating. Please tell me you have had this experience. I don't want to think that I am the only person ever to develop an intense attachment to a knife and fork.

People spend too much time cleaning up where they live. Other creatures — birds and animals — build their nest or den, make it comfortable, and sit down. Not humans. We sweep. We dust. We wash. Who knows what we have cleaned away that would be of interest to future generations.

I like to think of our houses as little time capsules. We would be misleading future generations if everything we left was neat and sanitized. Of course, they may struggle with their imaginations a bit to figure out why we kept all those old washcloths with holes in them or why we wore so many pairs of unmatched socks.

Even the places where we work tend to have become too sterile. I recently visited a newspaper office that looked like the set of a science-fiction movie. Computers and word processors were placed in little white cubicles all in one large room complete with metal furniture and fluorescent lights. I was glad to see that some obstinate reporters still had piles of newspapers stacked up in the corner of their cubicles. There is still hope.

Offices used to have "character," particularly newspaper offices that were populated by characters. There was no need for nameplates on the desk. You knew who occupied each desk by the identifiable clutter there.

I saw a sign somewhere that said, "Only sick minds can operate in a sterile environment." The writer was probably one of those old guys who thinks creativity can only find its spark in a cloud of cigarette smoke, overflowing wastebaskets, and piles of used paper cups. My kind of guy.

Creative people are always making notes about things that pop into their minds. How do you make notes on a computer? Oh, I know there are those palm-sized, electronic notepads that you can carry around in your pocket. But referring to "stored information" is not the same thing as smoothing out a crumpled piece of envelope and deciphering the scribbling made in the heat of inspiration.

I really don't like sloppiness. I'm as neat as the next guy (or the *next* anyway), but I can't understand why people spend so much time throwing away those things that make our lives interesting. We are a part of all we accumulate. If we don't throw it all away, we'll be bigger for it.

Horsing Around

I have been told I need to find another hobby. According to my wife, children, doctor, and banker, riding and keeping horses as a hobby no longer fits my lifestyle, health, or pocketbook.

If I really look at the situation objectively, I must agree with them. There was a time when I could get on a bareback horse without assistance — just grab a piece of mane and swing up. Now I must put the saddle on the horse if I am to mount him.

I used to look forward to riding a young horse that was a little rambunctious; that made me stay alert enough to avoid being dumped on the ground if the horse shied or bucked. I enjoyed testing my balance as we jumped over ditches, fallen trees, and even the white stripe on the side of the highway. If I failed to maintain my place on the horse's back, I would simply pick myself up and get back on. Now, if I fall off the horse, somebody else has to pick me up. That's why I keep my dependable old horse around.

Over the years I have made major contributions to the welfare of several veterinarians. Although I did as much as I could to take care of the various horse maladies that came along, there were many times when only a trained vet could take care of the situation. I have even paid a vet to euthanize a horse. Don't let anybody tell you it's easy to shoot a horse that has suffered a debilitating accident. It's worth it to have the doctor do the humane thing.

During my lifetime I have bought enough horse feed to have brought Napoleon's cavalry through the Russian winter in good shape. If I could weld together into a chain all the horseshoes I have bought, I would have enough chain to raise the *Titanic*.

I have used my creative ability to come up with appropriate insults each time a horse has stepped on me, kicked me, fallen on me, bitten me, or failed to respond to my directive to move or stop. Hopefully, God has forgiven me for such creativity.

If I could gather the cumulative dirt and manure that have been washed from my clothes and my body after cleaning horse stalls, I could fertilize Martha Stewart's whole lawn, as well as every flowerbed and window box.

On the other hand, there is no way to place a monetary value on my association with horses. It is impossible to measure the feeling of accomplishment that I have felt each time I raised a small foal, watched that animal grow into a beautiful steed, and saw the results of hours of work teaching him to respond to me.

There is a bond that develops between animals and humans who spend a lot of time together. That is particularly true when the animal is dependent on that human being for its welfare. All of the time spent together is not related to just the animal's health. The physical exercise of working with horses keeps the human's body fit as well.

But the greatest contribution a horse can make to a human's welfare is mental and emotional. A horse will listen when I complain about my day and never belittle my concern. When I ride a horse through the silence of the woods on a winter day, it's a therapy a psychiatrist's couch can't offer. When I walk back to the house from the barn after working with my horses, whether it was riding, grooming, or cleaning stalls, there is a contentment and welcomed weariness that come from the experience.

Maybe I should get another hobby. But I think I'll wait a little while longer.

The Family Farm

I t is with a great deal of sadness and reluctance that I must acknowledge the present decline and possibly the imminent demise of agriculture, or at least the dominance of agriculture in this country. Our standard of living, particularly in this part of our country, has been intertwined with the rise and fall of that portion of our economy.

It would be perpetuating a misconception if I did not point out the distinction between the various kinds of agriculture that have existed, have ceased to exist, and will continue to exist. The predominant method of farming that existed for most of our history was the family farm, a private enterprise run by individuals related by kinship. It is also that arrangement that has seen tremendous decline over the years. What remains and will continue are usually referred to as "corporate" farms, commercial entities that operate outside the generally perceived restrictions of smaller family farms.

Such an arrangement is not all bad. There are certain advantages to corporate farming. After all, it is a business, and corporate farms force the operators to make farming decisions based on good business practices. Those family farms that have survived have done so by adopting and adapting to new technology and business practices.

The increasing technology of farming has resulted in increased production of food. Such production has made food available to more people. I don't know exactly how much it is, but I do know that the United States produces much more than we can eat — so much more that sometimes a farmer will be paid not to grow a crop. Today's farmer must remember not only what he didn't grow but also what field he didn't grow it in.

At the same time, there are people in this country who go to sleep every night hungry because they don't have jobs to earn money to buy food. The increased technology has made the need for manual labor decrease. Ironically, sometimes it was the lack of available and affordable labor that led to the need to increase technology.

I am reminded of something an old farmer told me many years ago even while family farms were prevalent. He said, "Farming is a great way of life if you've got another way to make a living."

The family farm I remember was more than a way to make a living. It was a lifestyle that enabled a family to have the essentials of life — food, shelter, and clothing — and, if they were lucky, the money for other things, including advanced education for their children, many of whom would then leave the farm.

But along the way the family farm offered much more. It provided a close working relationship between family members. Fathers and sons, who worked together in the fields, had a special appreciation for each other because they understood how their work directly affected the other.

In addition, the family farm taught children to appreciate the value of money. Money earned by the sweat of their brow was much more valuable because it was their sweat and their money.

Growing up on a farm also provided children an understanding of the world around them: the changing seasons, the knowledge of the creation and passing of life — things you don't learn in a classroom or on the streets.

What made me think of all this was a comment I heard a little boy make in the grocery store the other day. He was standing at the "dairy" case where his mother was picking up a container of a dozen eggs. As he watched her, I saw him look at the "dairy" sign as he asked, "Mama, isn't a dairy where cows live?" The mother assured him that such was the case. He then asked, "What kind of cow gives eggs?"

I wonder how many other children will grow up never knowing where their food comes from. I feel sure that as the number of children raised on a farm decreases, the number who thinks cows give eggs will increase.

And that will be our loss, as well as theirs.

CHAPTER THREE

---

tar heel travels

On the Road

Since most of my working life has involved traveling around the state in an automobile, I believe I have accumulated enough experience to qualify as a good advisor on how to make the best of a bad traveling situation.

Growing up in a small town in southeastern North Carolina does not necessarily prepare anybody to be a traveler. In my early years I never had much of an inclination to go very far from home. A trip to Wilmington, 35 miles away, constituted a journey of some large proportion. When I was very young, my family did not have a car, which made a trip an even greater adventure. Even when we did own a car, there was not much reason to go far from Hallsboro. Not knowing what existed in faraway places negated any need to go there. As far as I was concerned, everything I needed was available in Hallsboro.

That opinion prevailed until I went off to college and discovered the world that existed outside the 35-mile excursions of my youth. Traveling on school trips broadened my horizons. But bus trips have a tendency not to have the intimacy with the countryside that you get with a car. It wasn't until I graduated from school and got a job that involved traveling solo in an automobile that I began to experience what the great state of North Carolina was all about.

So after more than 30 years of traveling by car throughout this state, I offer these suggestions.

Never go to a destination by the same route twice. After about the third time you have passed through an area, you stop paying attention to what you see. You begin to see what was there the last time you came through. You don't see the rolling pastures, the cloud-covered mountains, or sweeping vistas of the ocean. You only see the highway before you. Going by a different route will also disabuse you of the opinion that every gas station and convenience store is like every other. There are different people in each store.

Don't always eat at the same restaurants. There are hundreds of good places to eat in North Carolina. Don't judge the quality of the food by the outside of the building. Some of the best food I've ever eaten was at a little restaurant outside of Mebane that had once been a service station. They didn't change the décor much. My table was right beside where the grease pit used to be. They had just filled it up with dirt and put a concrete birdbath on it. No birds. But the food was excellent — fried pork chops, mashed potatoes, fried okra, and butter beans, as well as plenty of ice tea. Don't assume, however, that every place that looks so ordinary has good food. Sometimes a hog pen is only a hog pen.

Before you try a new restaurant, drive up as close to it as you can, roll down the window, and make sure it smells good. If it passes the smell test, proceed.

Don't trust anybody who does something for you and doesn't ask for a tip. Unless you are physically incapable of carrying your own luggage or trade-show equipment (particularly expensive cameras and such) don't use the services of a bellhop at the hotel. The next morning you may not have as much equipment to carry.

In fact, unless your meeting is at a hotel or you simply like to spend money, don't stay at a hotel. Lots of good motels are available, but be careful of those where the sign is missing a letter or two — like "S-ashore L-dge" or "Slee-tite I-n." If the owner won't fix the sign, he's not going to fix a lumpy mattress either.

Don't charge any phone calls to your room. I have stayed in places where my phone bill was more than the room charge. Call collect, go to a pay phone, or use a cell phone. Hotels must have a little telephone operator who gets paid by the call. I feel sure that the telephone company wouldn't charge the motel such an exorbitant rate.

By all means, go. There is so much to see and do and so many people to meet in this state, it would be a shame if you never went there.

The Little Piano Player

S everal years ago when I was in the television business, I was asked to be the emcee for a talent show held in a small eastern North Carolina town that shall remain nameless. The proceeds from the show were to go to the local fire and rescue squad, and the show itself was held in the fire station.

As is so often the case in small towns like this one, the evening's entertainment was part of a festival that included a parade and a beauty pageant. The beauty pageant had been held the night before the talent show, and the parade had been that afternoon.

When the lady who was the show chairwoman gave me the list of contestants and their introductions, I was impressed by the wide variety of talent to be judged. There were eight people in the contest, and their talents ranged from opera singing to aerobic dance. There was also an authentic Swiss yodeler on the program. So in my initial review of the evening's competition, I didn't see anything right away that I thought would be extraordinary. Was I ever wrong.

The first contestant was a little girl dressed like Shirley Temple. She came out and sang and danced to "The Good Ship Lollipop." She was pretty good and got a nice round of applause. I understand she had an extensive family in attendance.

Things were moving along pretty well as we listened to a fellow whistle his arrangement of "Listen to the Mockingbird," a lady play a rhythmic tune with the same spoons she had used to fix supper the previous evening, and another lady sing her rendition of "How Great Thou Art" accompanied by her husband playing the saw. (The saw is played with a violin bow while the saw is placed between the knees of the player.)

While I enjoyed these performances much as I had enjoyed watching "Ted Mack's Amateur Hour" on television, I didn't see any performers who should quit their day jobs.

Then a little girl named Reba came out to play the piano. The piano itself was most interesting. It was one of those old heavy uprights, and a few of the keys had been chipped. She came out dressed in a frilly, white dress and little, white, patent leather shoes. She was probably 10 years old. Her red hair had been curled so tightly on her head she looked like she was wearing a shower cap with bumps on it.

Reba sat down to play "Moonlight Sonata." She hesitantly played a few notes, then stopped and began to cry. The audience was silent, evidently feeling sorry for the little girl. I started to ask for some applause and help her off stage when an elderly gentleman came from backstage and sat down on the piano bench beside the little girl. I don't know what he said, but the little girl stopped crying and began to play the piano again. She began tentatively but grew more confident, and the elderly gentleman continued to whisper to her as she played. She finished the piece to great applause, curtsied to the audience, took the gentleman's hand, and left the stage.

Now if this story were to follow the Hollywood formula, the little girl would have won the contest; but she didn't. A young man who played his fiddle arrangement of "The Devil Went Down to Georgia" won.

I left the town and hadn't heard from anyone there until the other day when I attended a wedding in a little country church near Wallace. The church was full, and I got there a little late. As soon as I saw the minister, I thought he looked familiar. At the reception I talked to him and found out that he was the old gentleman who had helped the little girl at the talent contest. I asked him what had become of the little girl. He told me she was his granddaughter. He had been her piano teacher, and she was the organist for the wedding.

The girl had already left so I didn't get to talk to her, but I remembered that talent contest at the fire station. The fiddler may have won the prize, but the little girl and her grandfather won my heart.

Snow Job

I have always thought that merchandising was a matter of finding out what people want and providing it to them at a reasonable price. I have recently had occasion to revise the "reasonable price" part.

If somebody wants something and it is presented to them at the right time and in the right place, they will pay whatever the traffic will bear. During a particularly warm autumn, I witnessed this truism.

Apparently, some folks cannot wait for cold weather and will jump at any chance to accelerate the approach of winter. Evidently, there was a convention of those folks meeting down at Wrightsville Beach, and an enterprising young man took advantage of the time and the place.

When I first saw him, I thought he was an ordinary snow cone vendor with some snow cones left over from Labor Day. But as I got close enough to read the sign he had placed in front of his machine, I saw that this was a real salesman with a touch of imagination.

The sign read, "Authentic Minnesota Snowballs. Fresh Daily. $1 Each."

Needless to say, I was intrigued by the unique sales promotion, so I pulled my car over and walked to the snowball stand.

"Real snowballs?" I asked.

"Authentic," was the reply.

"You must have gotten a whole planeful to be able to sell them for only a dollar apiece," I said.

"Oh, I didn't fly them in. I use an old family recipe for snowballs handed down for generations by my family in Minnesota," he said.

"I didn't know there was a recipe for snowballs. I thought you picked up some snow off the ground and made it into a snowball."

"Oh, no. That shows how much you Southerners know about snow. To get Minnesota snowballs, you have to get a starter ball from a family member in Minnesota. Then you mix it with fresh snow, or you can use snow that has been in your freezer at home. You have to be sure the right amount of authentic Minnesota snow is mixed in each ball.

"You see, Minnesota snow is unique, and it has the ability to reproduce itself if it is exposed to other snow in the right percentage. Minnesota snow is regenerative and dominates other snow."

"How do you know how much Minnesota snow to mix with our local snow?" I asked.

"Oh, I can't tell you that. It's a secret recipe that came to America more than a hundred years ago when my great-grandmother came to Minnesota from Sweden. In fact, there is a Viking curse that says that anyone who discloses the secret recipe to anyone outside the family will be sent into permanent exile in some warm and balmy climate."

"Are you having any luck selling your snowballs?" I asked.

"Oh, yes. This has been a good market this year. Most of my customers are folks who moved here from one of the Northern states and are really homesick for authentic snowballs."

"Whatever gave you the idea that you could make money selling snowballs down here in North Carolina?"

"To tell you the truth, I was inspired by a friend of mine from college. He was a native North Carolinian, and one year he went home with me for Christmas in Minnesota. On the way, we stopped and picked some cotton in a field off Interstate 95. When we got home he sold every bit we had, one small piece at a time, for a dollar apiece."

"Where is your friend now?"

"He's in Minnesota selling cotton, and I'm here in North Carolina selling snowballs. We get together at Christmas and divide the profits."

They were both in the right place at the right time.

What's Going On

I did not know the man's name. Still don't. He was standing in front of the little convenience store just outside Kinston on N.C. Highway 11.

I had stopped there to get my usual afternoon snack of a Mountain Dew and a pack of Nabs. As I started to open the door to the establishment, the man spoke to me.

"Hey, buddy, want to buy a paper?" he said.

I said, "No, thank you," and continued into the store.

It didn't take me long to get my Mountain Dew and pack of Nabs, maybe 10 minutes. Just as I came out the door the man said, "Still got a paper if you need it."

My curiosity was about to get the best of me, so I said, "What kind of paper you got?"

"Today's," he said.

"I mean what's the name of the paper."

"I don't know," he replied. "I can't read. I thought you looked like a man what would read a paper, so I figured you might want one."

I looked at the man a little closer. He was neatly dressed: a pair of tan pants and matching shirt, a good pair of work shoes, and a baseball-type cap with a Confederate flag on the front. He didn't look like the typical panhandler, and I wondered why he was trying to sell me a paper he couldn't read.

So I asked him, "Why are you trying to sell me a paper you can't read yourself?"

"Everybody always asks me that," he said. "I always tell them the same thing."

That's all he said. I waited a while and asked the inevitable follow-up question, "And what is that?"

"My daddy died when I was just a baby. Didn't leave nothing but an old run-down house and a sorry piece of land for me and my mama. She finally sold it all to pay what we owed and we moved into town.

"She went to work taking care of other people's houses, cleaning and washing, taking care of children and all. One time she went to work for a fellow in Kinston. He had a real nice house, drove a nice car. I was real impressed with what all that man had. So I asked Mama how that man made all his money. She said he was in the newspaper business. Right then I knew that was my calling."

I chuckled to myself at the simple-mindedness of the man. I smugly asked him, "You can't make much money selling one paper at a time, can you?"

"How else you gonna do it?" he asked. "A body can't read but one paper at a time. There ain't but one news and that's today's. What happened yesterday is history, and what happens tomorrow is just maybe."

"Do you ever have anybody read the news to you?" I asked.

"Naw," he said. "If anything important is going to happen right close by, somebody will tell me. If it ain't close enough to bother me, I figure I don't need to know it anyhow."

I bought the newspaper from the man. I couldn't argue with his logic. One of my frequent statements to anybody who will listen is that "Everything in the world is personal."

Whether he knew it or not, that man had just told me why there will always be a need for local newspapers: to tell us what's going on that is really worth knowing about.

Dog Food

We have all seen those folks standing beside the road with a sign that says, "Will work for food." I am sympathetic toward these unfortunate people, but since I am usually in a car several miles from home, I am not really able to provide any assistance to them at the time.

I always feel a little guilty for not helping them because I am reminded of the old proverb, "There but for the grace of God go I." I am sure there are others who share this sentiment, who feel as lucky or as blessed as I do.

That was the thought that came to my mind as I approached an intersection near Greenville the other day. I was almost half-a-mile away when I saw the man standing by the road holding up a piece of cardboard. I couldn't read what was written on the cardboard, but I supposed it was that familiar statement requesting work for food.

As I got closer and began to slow down to stop for the red light at that intersection, I noticed a black dog lying on the ground next to where the man was standing. About the same time, I was able to read the words on the sign the man was holding. They said, "Will work to feed my dog."

Naturally, I was taken aback by the sign. In fact, I was so stunned that I kept looking at the man, the dog, and the sign even after the light changed. The honking of car horns behind me brought me out of my trance, and I moved on. But I hadn't gone too far when my curiosity got the best of me. So I turned the car around and went back to the intersection.

I parked the car at a convenience store across the road from the man and his dog. I walked over to the gentleman and introduced myself and told him that I was curious why his sign was worded as it was.

He was quick to respond. He said, "You'd be surprised how many people will stop and give me money to buy dog food but don't offer to give me any work to do."

I voiced my skepticism. "You're kidding, aren't you?" I said.

"No," he reiterated. "People will hand me money through their car window and tell me to use the money to buy the dog some food, then they drive away."

I asked him if that made him feel bad or did he think people didn't care about him.

He said, "No, I don't hold it against them. I take their money, and I buy human food and share it with my dog."

I told him I was passing through and didn't live in the area so I wasn't in a position to offer him any work, but I did give him $10 and told him to buy some food for himself and his dog.

As I got back in my car and headed on down the road, I continued to think about the pair I had left behind. Was that a case of a man using the dog as a gimmick to panhandle food or was he really placing the dog's welfare ahead of his own? How long did it take the man to figure out that he could get more money by presenting the dog as the needy one?

Beyond my skepticism regarding the situation, I began to think about what the situation said about the rest of us. What would cause folks to care more about the welfare of a dog than they did a human being?

I didn't reach any conclusion, but my best guess is that regardless of what the circumstances were that caused the man to be in the shape he was in, most people figured he could still provide in some way for himself — even if he just stood by the side of the road with his sign. The dog couldn't.

Too Good to Be True

During a recent ice/snow storm, I found it necessary to travel and was not looking forward to it. I don't even like to drive in the rain. Nevertheless, I headed north through the farmlands of eastern North Carolina. The roads were slippery; just enough precipitation was falling to keep my windshield icy, and traffic was heavy enough to keep me tense.

Somewhere near Smithfield my car made a noise that caused me considerable consternation. Although all the dials on the dash said everything was all right, I knew the noise was an indication that such was not the case.

I had to make a speaking engagement in Wilson at noon, however, so I didn't stop, hoping that the noise would go away. It didn't.

I made it to the meeting in Wilson and directly after the meeting sought out a garage. There was not a lot to choose from as I headed back down U.S. Highway 301. But just before getting to Kenly, I saw a handwritten sign that said, "We fix all kinds of cars." My motto is "any port in a storm," so I turned off the highway onto a small rural road and drove about a mile.

Then I saw it. It looked like something from the old television show "The Dukes of Hazzard." It was a tin building with several junked cars around it. Smoke was coming from the tin flue of a wood-burning stove in the back corner of the building. I could see the figure of a man bent over the fender of a car with the hood up. I figured he was the man who could "fix all kinds of cars."

As it turned out, he was. He was a jovial fellow clad in coveralls. He had about a three-day stubble of beard on his face and a plug of chewing tobacco tucked in one side of his mouth.

As I approached him he straightened up, wiped his hands on a cloth he pulled from his back pocket, and said, "Howdy, friend. What can I do for you?"

I told him about the noise the car was making and he opened the hood. He immediately determined that the power steering was about to malfunction. (He didn't say "malfunction." His actual terminology can't be printed in a family book.) He also told me he didn't have the parts to fix it, but he could give me some temporary relief until I could get to the dealership in Smithfield. I told him I would appreciate that.

While he was working on the car, he asked where I was from. I told him, and he said, "I used to know a girl down there when I was stationed at Fort Bragg. Never did go to her house, though. She used to come up to the base every weekend to see her brother, and we got pretty friendly."

Trying to keep the conversation going, I said, "I'll bet she was like most of the girls down home, real good-looking."

"Nope," he said. "She was kinda homely looking, to tell you the truth. But a good ol' country girl. She talked to me, told me all about her family having a farm down there and everything. I got to liking her pretty good."

"Y'all struck up a friendship, huh?"

"Yeah. She'd leave home before daybreak, I guess, to come see me — and her brother. I liked her. But mainly I liked the food she brought with her. She brought stuff the Army didn't have. Stuff like collards and neck-bones, and she'd bring pork skins that her daddy made at hog killings. And every once in a while she'd bring a little homemade wine and cakes and pies. I tell you, me and her brother ate good."

"Now, you gonna tell me you married that girl," I said.

"Oh, no," he replied. "A woman who can cook like that would be way too popular. I'd have to always be looking out for men coming 'round the house hunting her cooking. It just ain't good policy to marry a woman who cooks too good. I heard folks say not to marry a good-looking woman 'cause she liable to run around on ya. But I tell ya, good looks'll fade away. Good cooking just gets better with time."

Country Roads

Weeds grow quickly on old farm roads. Nothing impedes their growth — no modern vehicle traffic, no plethora of pedestrians tramp it down. Its most frequent traffic is old dogs, some in singular pursuit of romance and some in packs scavenging for a meal.

Most people don't care where these roads lead since people with a destination have no reason to follow them. But if we look carefully, we can see ourselves along these roads. Our ancestors came down these roads, not only those from centuries ago but recent kin — grandparents and great-grandparents, the aunts and uncles we used to see at family reunions. We listened to their stories and saw in our minds what took place along these roads.

These were wagon roads long before the automobile and pickup truck were invented. The wagons came to little houses built by the hands of the people who lived in them. No contractor was needed to build their home. The wagons brought their spartan furniture, often handmade — shuck-bottom chairs and three-legged stools, butter churns, beds with rope springs, and tables made of three wide boards.

The most lasting thing the roads brought was people. The roads ran a long way from town. It may not seem like a great distance today, but if you had to walk or ride a wagon to get there, it could be "a fer piece."

If we take the time and make the effort to traverse these country roads today, we see only the remnants of a life that was once bursting at the seams with agriculture. It was a life literally built from the ground up. The soil grew not only crops, but also a spirit of independence that we took for granted until it was gone.

For most of North Carolina, tobacco was the heart of the economy. It could provide a decent income for families who didn't have a lot of land. For a long time, this labor-intensive operation didn't lack for workers. Families were big, and there were plenty of people available who needed the work.

But now those roads that saw the wagons and trucks loaded with neatly tied bundles of tobacco have no traffic. Much of society has said that the very item that sustained life for those farm families caused the death of others. So the roads are empty.

The roads that provided access to a new life for those long-ago families are the same roads that so many of today's farm families travel as they leave those farms. Modern agriculture has no place for the small family farm. The transition to mass pork and poultry production has peaked, and the other alternatives are few. Although they may be riding in their cars and trucks, it's still a long trip to town.

The floods and hurricanes of the past few years have washed away much of the soil that once nourished those fields of tobacco. Those roads are flooded now by the recent storms, the water rushing across them at the small bridges that span the creeks and streams.

An old man stood on the porch of the country store and told the traveler about the effect of the floods on the farmland around the area. He pointed out the devastation of the crops, the loss of livestock, and the destruction of property. Then he summed up the plight of the farmer, a situation not much understood by people who had not traveled those country roads. "Heck, it don't matter. I couldn't make a living on it no more anyhow. Then again, I ain't never tried growing rice."

To that farmer and those who are faced with seemingly insurmountable obstacles, I offer this prayer, which is on a bronze plaque as a memorial to (and written by) Robert Louis Stevenson in St. Giles Cathedral in Edinburgh, Scotland:

> *Give us grace and strength to forebear and persevere. ...*
> *Give us courage and gaiety and the quiet mind, spare*
> *to us our friends, soften to us our enemies.*

✄ ✄ ✄

CHAPTER FOUR

----

real characters

✄ ✄ ✄

Vila's Place

Every time I ride by the old place, I am reminded of Vila. The building that was once a small café has been remodeled and appears to be just an outbuilding of the house where Vila used to live.

Her little café was a local landmark at Lake Waccamaw, as well as a popular place to eat. She only served breakfast and lunch, and both times of the day would find the place full of people, a wide spectrum of community folks.

Twenty years ago, down on the edge of the Great Green Swamp, there were not too many eating establishments to choose from. So, apart from the fact that the food was good and plentiful, almost everybody ate at Vila's at one time or another.

Of course, there were the regulars. Traveling salesmen made a point of getting to Lake Waccamaw about noon. The foresters from the Forest Service and the paper companies met there. Many retired men chose breakfast with Vila instead of imposing on their wives or making their own. Several men who worked in other towns got up early enough to have breakfast at Vila's before driving to work.

She always served them a hearty meal — bacon and eggs or ham and eggs for breakfast with plenty of coffee. And grits, of course.

Lunch was also good country fare. Vila had a menu, but it was purely superfluous. Everybody ate whatever she had prepared on any given day. Sometimes it was chicken — fried, baked, boiled, chicken salad — with rice and gravy, beans, macaroni and cheese, fried okra. Stew beef and rice was a frequent dish. Everything was always good.

But it wasn't just the food that kept people coming back to Vila's. Vila was a unique woman who carried on a continuous conversation with her customers. Short and buxom, she genuinely liked cooking for the men who frequented her café. And the customers liked Vila in return.

Sometimes her humor was a little ribald, but that appealed to the clientele. They knew she was really interested in them and how the wives and children were doing. If she heard that a family member was sick, she'd take food to them.

As a sign of appreciation, deer hunters would often bring venison to Vila to cook for her customers. Such an act once led to an incident that really defines Vila.

Upon hearing that Vila's lunch special was venison, the local game warden decided to try the dish, knowing it was against the law for a commercial establishment to sell uninspected wild game. He ordered the venison, ate it, and went to pay for his meal. He asked, "How much was the venison?"

Vila replied, "Not a thing. It's absolutely free."

A little surprised, the game warden realized he couldn't charge Vila, so he said "thank you" and started to put his wallet back in his pocket.

"But that glass o' tea'll be $3.50," said Vila.

Everybody in the café laughed. The game warden paid for the tea and continued to eat lunch there nearly every day along with all the other regulars. Kind of a peaceable kingdom.

Back to School

My friend Marvin is in his early 80s. He looks it. He has led the kind of life most of us would not want. But he has come through it without any regrets and with a wisdom that extends beyond the boundaries of that accumulated solely by aging.

I met Marvin at one of the many civic club conventions I attend as part of my job. The first thing I noticed was his bright red hair. It was combed — no, bonded — to his head by enough hair cream to stop up every sink in North Carolina. There was not a lot of hair to work with, but he had made a little pompadour right in the front that gave him a certain amount of distinction.

Of course, because of his hair color, nobody called him Marvin. "Red" was the name he had been called since he played baseball back in high school. "I wanted to be a professional baseball player, but I had to get a job right after I got out of high school," he said. "I was good enough to play professionally, but back then baseball players didn't make all that much money, and it wasn't the most secure way to make a living."

Red left the Sandhills of North Carolina looking for employment. Unlike many others at the time, he headed south instead of north and wound up in the steel mills of Birmingham, Alabama. Heat affected every part of his life. "Alabama gets hotter than North Carolina in the summertime, and you add the heat of that steel mill, and it will make you think Hades would be a relief. Even the floor of the mill was so hot it'd make the soles of your shoes smoke."

When World War II came, Red left the steel mills and joined the Army. "They wanted me to stay. Said the country was going to need more steel for the war. Offered me more money. But I figured if I was going to give my life for my country, I'd rather get shot by the Japanese than die in that darn mill."

He was in the Pacific through the entire war. He helped build strips for planes to land on the tiny islands where much of the fighting took place. "We'd have to do some fighting ourselves every once in a while. Zeros would fly over and spray us; we'd run for cover and stay there 'til they were gone, then we'd get right back to work. That makes for a long war."

After the war he stayed in the Army and was sent to Korea. "Apart from the fighting in Korea, the main thing I remember was the cold. As much as I hated that steel-mill heat, I hated that Korean cold more."

Red was wounded in Korea. After his wounds healed he was discharged and came back home to North Carolina. After spending some time just lying around home, he decided to head for the Carolina coast. At Southport he got a job on a fishing boat, but when tobacco season rolled around, he went to work for one of the auction houses. When the season ended, one of the tobacco companies asked if he wanted to go to the Kentucky market. He said he did, and he stayed with that company until he retired in 1985.

The day after he retired he asked a travel agent to set up a bus tour around the country for him. "I had always wanted to see this country I had fought for. I didn't want to drive and didn't know exactly where to go." For the next several years, Red took bus trips around the country, visited relatives, and "just about bored myself to death.

"I saw a lot of college campuses in my traveling, and every time I'd go by one I'd think about my lack of education," he said. So at the age of 79 Red went to college. "I'm still going to the community college here. I may never live long enough to graduate, but I'm enjoying the process. It sure beats the heck outta working in a steel mill. Besides, life's not over 'til you're dead."

Working for Peanuts

The boy had parked his pickup truck right at the exit of the mall parking lot. Like all good businesses, location was very important. His business was selling boiled peanuts, and by parking at the exit folks had to stop before pulling out on the highway. This location gave him a chance to hawk his peanuts.

I watched him as he positioned his truck so the tailgate was facing the mall parking lot. He brought out a gigantic umbrella, opened it, and pressed the staff down into the sandy soil between the sidewalk and the street. It was a garish red, yellow, and blue colored thing that would be hard to ignore.

Then he brought out his peanuts. He had some already packaged in little paper bags with the top corners twisted to keep them closed. He pulled a big steel pot up to the edge of the tailgate and carefully unwrapped a piece of burlap that had been tied to cover the top of the pot. As he removed the burlap, I could see the steam come out of the top, indicating that the peanuts had recently been cooked and had probably been soaking for a while.

He immediately sat down beside the steel pot and placed a small stack of little paper bags on the other side of him. He began to fill the bags, taking big handfuls first, then topping each bag with three or four very full peanuts. As he completed filling and twisting the top of each bag, he added it to the neat stack beside those already bagged.

He was doing this smoothly, not in a hurry; you could tell this was a familiar task. He soon had a good-sized pile of bagged peanuts, so he sat with his back against the side of the truck and began to eat some of the peanuts out of the pot.

I had often said that if I were a boiled-peanut vendor, I would never make any money because I would eat up all the profit. It appeared that this young man was facing the same fate.

But I noticed that after he ate each peanut, he would carefully place the two halves of the shell back together so it looked like a full peanut. He would place the hollow shells neatly beside him, and periodically he would carefully pick them up and put all the empty shells in a little bag and twist the corners.

I thought I was watching a little fraud in progress. From where I sat, the bags filled with empty shells looked just like the full bags.

I walked over to him and asked for a bag of peanuts. I paid the exorbitant price of $1.25 for one of the little bags. As I stood there and ate them, I struck up a conversation with the young man. He was very congenial. I asked him how was business.

"Pretty good," he said. "It's early yet. I'll get busy about lunchtime. I been thinking of bringing some soft drinks like Co' Cola or Mountain Dew out here. Peanuts are good and salty. Folks might want a drink with them. But then, most folks just get right back in their car and go on."

As I stood there eating the peanuts, I thought I might explore the fraudulent practice of selling the empty shells in the little bags. So I asked him, "Do you charge the same for these bags (indicating the empty shells) as you do for the rest of them?"

"Oh, no," he said. "I keep those to tally up in the evening. Mama said I could eat all I wanted, but I had to keep track of them, so that's what I do. I put the empty shells in the bags, and at the end of the day I have to pay for what I ate and Mama counts the bags."

I was surprised to find an honest man. Diogenes would have been pleased.

The Pink Rocking Chair

My friend J.B. had wanted me to come by to see him, so I did. It wasn't easy getting to his house. I had to leave the paved road and follow the sandy Onslow County road about a mile through some cut-over woodland and across a wooden bridge his father had built back in the 1920s.

He had told me, "Papa built that bridge when he bought his first car. Didn't need a bridge for a mule and wagon. Built it out of solid oak boards he cut right here on the farm." Those same boards were still there, give or take a board or two, for me to cross that day.

When I crossed the bridge, I could see J.B. out in the front yard of his little house. It was the house he had been born in almost 90 years ago. When he was 15 years old, he had left it and his family there near Hubert to follow the horse-show circuit as a groom for a wealthy man from Jacksonville. During that time he had done well for himself financially, saving his money and making good investments. He had come back home upon retirement. I had asked him once why, with all his money, he hadn't retired to Florida or some place other than Hubert. "I saw all I wanted to see of Florida and most everywhere else. I hadn't seen enough of home," he answered.

As I got out of the car and started toward the house, I could see that J.B. was painting a rocking chair. He had placed it on two cement blocks right out in the yard and was applying the paint with a small paintbrush. The color of the paint was pink.

I thought it was curious that this man would want a pink rocking chair for that particular house. The sides of the house had turned gray from weather and age. The porch that went across the front of the house was about three feet off the ground, and you could see under it where a couple of dogs were resting. Only one of the front windows, the one for the bedroom, had any curtains.

J.B. looked a lot like the house. What hair he had was gray, and he wore a pair of gray corduroy slacks, a faded white shirt with the sleeves rolled up, and an old pair of lace-up riding boots.

We greeted each other, shook hands, and he invited me to come and sit on the porch with him. I wanted to ask him right then why he was painting that rocking chair pink but was afraid it might embarrass him, and I figured if he wanted me to know he'd tell me later.

He poured himself a glass of water from a jar filled with ice water and asked me if I wanted some. I told him I did. J.B. had told me long ago that he believed in drinking a lot of water. No soft drinks and definitely no alcohol. He said that was one reason he was still healthy at his age.

We talked for a good while about the business he had called to talk about. He reminisced for a while, as always when we were together, about the old days when he was traveling as a groom for the wealthy man's horses.

I was ready to leave and as we walked toward the car, he asked, "Aren't you going to ask me about the pink rocking chair?"

"Well, I am curious," I said. "But I figured you'd tell me if you wanted me to know."

"I knew you wouldn't ask. You are one of the few people who ever come to see me, so I'll tell you. Hardly anybody ever comes up here to talk to me. I figure that when I die folks will come up here and find this pink rocking chair. They will wonder why an old man like me would have a piece of furniture that color. They will speculate and propose all kinds of reasons, none of which will be true. I painted it so they will have something to talk about and remember me when I'm gone even if they wouldn't talk to me when I was living."

J.B. died a few months after my visit. I went to his funeral and, sure enough, the main topic of conversation at the graveside service was the pink rocking chair. I never told anybody his reason for painting the chair.

Gone Fishing

She was just a little girl, no more than seven years old. Her "big" brother, probably 10 years old, stood beside her on the bank of the big ditch that ran out of the Green Swamp and into a creek that fed Lake Waccamaw. They were sharing the warm autumn afternoon "drowning worms" as they pushed their fishing poles over the dark water.

She was seated on a little wooden stool that kept sinking in the soft dirt of the ditchbank. Periodically, she'd stand up and pull the stool out of the dirt, rearrange it to suit herself, and sit back down. Each time she'd stand up, she'd lay the pole on the ground.

It appeared that she had tried to dress as much like her brother as she could. They both wore jeans, T-shirts, and sneakers. But they still didn't look alike. She had white-blonde hair and wore steel-rimmed glasses that kept sliding down her nose. To push the glasses back up on her nose, she once again had to put the fishing pole on the ground. She couldn't hold it with one hand. Between repositioning her stool and fixing her glasses, she spent most of her time putting down and picking up the fishing pole.

Her brother was never more than two steps away from her. He would look over at her each time she moved, but he never spoke a word. Every once in a while he'd pull the baited hook out of the water and reposition it. He didn't cast it, just moved it a bit.

As I watched the two, the little girl pulled her hook out of the water and swung it over to the boy. He reached in his can and placed another worm on the hook. They still hadn't spoken a word.

I could see the two from the porch of the house, where I was reading a magazine. As I read I would look up to see if they were still there. For almost two hours they stayed there, never catching a fish or even getting a bite.

As the late afternoon sun began to set and the two came under the shade of the cypress trees along the bank, I heard an exclamation from their direction. The boy had a bite.

I could see him pulling the pole up from the water and backing up from the ditchbank.

I could also hear him saying, "Molly, Molly, come git a-holt of it!"

The little girl dropped her fishing pole and ran to her brother, and the two of them grabbed the pole. About that time the fish came out of the water. I don't know what kind it was. They were too far away for me to tell, but it was a small fish and it was working diligently to disengage itself from the hook.

The two managed to get the fish on the bank, and I saw the boy reach down, pick the fish up, and remove the hook from its mouth. Then he did the most remarkable thing. He reached down and got his sister's fishing pole, took her hook, and placed it in the fish's mouth. He gave her the pole, and the two of them kept turning the cane pole until the fishing line had pulled the fish up to the end of the pole.

Then the boy picked up his pole, tied the hook end to the pole, and began walking off with his sister beside him, her cane pole over her shoulder and the small fish hanging from the tip.

I wonder who got credit for catching the fish.

Cold House, Warm Hearts

S hortly after Christmas, I went to see some old friends of mine who live down at the edge of the Green Swamp in Brunswick County. I got to know Cleatus and Emily Simmons back when Cleatus was hauling pulpwood to the paper mill at Rieglewood. He is now retired and doesn't get around too well because of arthritis.

I knew that it was close to the date of their wedding anniversary, but I didn't know the exact date or how many years they had been married. At the time I went to see them we sat out on the porch because the weather was still relatively warm for the time of year, and the state of the weather was our first topic of conversation.

"We ain't even had a fire this year," said Emily. "Although sometimes at night we put an extra quilt on the bed."

I noticed that Cleatus had a big pile of firewood stacked up between two pine trees in the yard. "Looks like you're prepared for cold weather when it does come," I commented.

"Oh, yeah. I like to stay warm," he said. "To tell you the truth, if it'd been this warm 60 years ago this week, me and Emily probably wouldn't have gotten married."

Even as the two laughed, I could see a slight blush come to Emily's face. It was easy to see they still had that special bond that comes with being married to each other for so long.

"That wasn't what you said 60 years ago, Cleatus Simmons. You was a smooth talker back then. Why, he used to make up little poems and say them to me. He couldn't read or write too good, but he could make up the poems and recite them to me — make them rhyme and everything. I thought that was right sweet of him. He used to tell me my hair reminded him of corn silk and all such stuff as that. Now he'd probably tell me it looks more like the moss on a cypress tree."

Again there was that easy laughter.

"Did he court you a long time before you got married, Emily?" I asked.

"He come around a lot before we was actually courting. I wasn't but 14 and Cleatus was 18, and my daddy didn't think too much about us actually keeping company. We didn't leave the homeplace by ourselves 'til I was 16, and we went to the show (movies) down to Southport. It wasn't but about six months after that that we got married."

"I think she married me for my money," joked Cleatus. "I was working for Mr. Clemmons down at his sawmill making 10 cents a day. He let me use scrap lumber to build our first house."

Emily said, "And that was the coldest house we ever lived in. We had an old tin stove, and we'd fill that full of pine boards and we were warm long as it lasted. But when the fire went out, sometimes at night I thought I'd freeze."

Cleatus added, "Sometimes I'd let it go out on purpose. All our children was born in September, you know." As Cleatus laughed, Emily blushed and turned her head aside as she laughed with him.

Cleatus went on to say, "Now sometimes the cold was rough on me out to the sawmill. And when I started pulpwooding, seems like the cold would make the wood harder to cut. I'd come home past dark and wore out and Emily'd put the babies to bed and rub my feet with hot, wet towels to thaw them out."

"From the looks of things, cold weather didn't hurt you," I said.

"Nope," said Cleatus. "We always had warm hearts."

Clara Mae's Magic Touch

C lara Mae used to work for my grandmother during tobacco season. She worked at the barn during the harvest as a "stringer," tying the leaves on the sticks to be hung in the barn. Later, she would work in the pack house tying the cured leaves into bundles to be placed on short sticks prior to stacking for sale at the warehouse.

Now, after nearly 40 years, it's not Clara Mae's expertise with tobacco I remember. I remember how she was known as a healer. She could heal anything, but her most popular curative had to do with the removal of warts. I don't remember the exact procedure, but it involved placing a leaf of some kind moistened with chewing tobacco spittle on the wart and the saying of some words as she passed her hand over the afflicted area.

When I knew Clara Mae, it never occurred to me that she was a "conjure woman." I thought she possessed some kind of magic medicine that the doctors in town didn't have or even knew about. Some of the black folks called her "doctor."

It was some time during my teenage years that a black friend of mine told me that Doctor Clara Mae could "talk the fire out" of burns. He had personal knowledge of this ability because his mother had called Clara Mae to his house when his little sister had accidentally placed her hand on the hot wood stove in their living room. He said that Clara Mae had given him a little bag of items along with some salve to place on the child's hand.

The little bag had contained an assortment of small animal bones and dried leaves. The bag was to be tied around the child's neck and left there for a month. According to my friend, the burn healed without even a scar.

Even after hearing all this, I figured Clara Mae somehow had access to medicine that "regular" doctors didn't have. It wasn't until sometime in the early 1970s that I met a man from Beaufort, South Carolina, who told me that such practices were "voodoo."

I had always thought that voodoo was something you only saw in the movies and that it was only practiced in places like Haiti or New Orleans. I had heard the folk songs about Marie Laveau, the Witch of the Bayous, who would charm people into the swamps and rob and kill them. In the movies, there was always at least one chicken death and a lot of dancing by firelight and somebody usually stuck pins in a voodoo doll that represented a person who was being "hexed."

But the gentleman from Beaufort had been a sheriff down in that part of the country and had seen the results of voodoo practices first-hand. In fact, because it became such a big part of his law enforcement activity, he had become something of an expert on the subject.

After talking to this sheriff, I mentioned the conversation to another black friend who worked at my family's store. His first reaction was, "Boy, you don't want nothing to do with no conjuring unless you're real sick." Later, he told me he knew Clara Mae and that she had been to his house when his wife's blood "weren't right." He said Clara Mae had found that his wife's blood was "too sweet," and she had to take "root medicine" every morning to get it back where it should be.

Clara Mae may have been a conjure woman, but I never saw her flinging chicken blood all over the place or chanting anything. She didn't fit any of the stereotypes I had come to associate with voodoo. She seemed like a very nice lady who was able to heal people. Like all stereotypes there is always some flaw in drawing the picture. In Clara Mae's case the flaw was that she was a white woman. In any case, I know she could get rid of warts because she got rid of one of mine.

Breakfast of Patriots

As always in a time of national crisis, I turn to the most authoritative assembly of experts on the subject to find the best answer to whatever the problem may be. This assemblage is easy to find. The group is always present for breakfast at almost any diner or café in every small town in America.

The ancient Greeks sought out an oracle, someone recognized as wise and authoritative. An oracle was often a priest or priestess. With few exceptions, these modern-day oracles are not privy to divine guidance in arriving at their opinions.

That is not to say that these "sages of the diner" are not well informed about their subject. In fact, it amazes me to see how, in just a few weeks, so much knowledge can been acquired about countries such as Iraq, Pakistan, Afghanistan, and other heretofore-unknown nations. To most of us gathered around the café table, Kabul was a stone used to pave streets until we read up on it in *Newsweek*. We can now tell you about the theological and social background of the perpetrators who committed those insidious acts of violence on September 11, 2001. We may not know for sure, but it sure beats not knowing anything at all.

I say "we" here because I find myself entering into these conversations as if I, too, know much more than I did before September 11. I listen intently to the news broadcasts. I hang on every word of the reports and then mentally take notes as expert after expert is trotted out to explain what the news really is. (I wonder how many journalism school curricula include News Analysis 101.) Unfortunately, I begin to do my own analysis by asking questions and seeking answers based on my own recently acquired expertise.

For instance, if a man is so smart that he can successfully plan and execute one of the most evil and violent acts ever perpetrated on American soil, why is he living in a cave?

If some of those guys wearing turbans never cut their hair (as reported by Peter Jennings), how much cloth is there in proportion to hair as the whole coiffure rests on their heads?

Of course, I never pose those kinds of questions to the guys at the café. Although I'm sure they could give me an answer, I am much more interested in their opinion as to how they would conduct this seek-and-destroy mission against worldwide terrorism. Most of the members of the café forum are veterans of a war. They know what it takes to defeat an enemy. I sit in awe as they recall the perilous fights in which they either participated or helped develop in those past wars. These are the members of the "Greatest Generation." They are, in all honesty, still my heroes. Most of them would jump right in the fight today if they could summon back their youth.

But we are told in the news reports that this is a different kind of fight. How can we understand this enemy who doesn't share our value for human life? "In 'our' war we had to deal with kamikaze pilots. In this war, they're all kamikazes," one veteran said. "It's gonna be like trying to get rid of fire ants. We can run them out of one hole and they'll just turn up in another."

As I listened to those men talk, I wondered if President Bush could benefit from their counsel. I'm sure they would be glad to give him advice. He needs all he can get.

The Art of Whittling

The old man said he was a whittler, not a wood carver. He said this in response to my question as to what he was carving. He was sitting on a soft-drink crate turned up on its edge under the shelter of a makeshift produce shed. There was a soft breeze blowing off the marsh nearby. Although several people had stopped to buy some of the watermelons, cantaloupes, tomatoes, and shrimp in an open box, he didn't interrupt his whittling to tend to them.

"You see," he said, "carving means when I start out I got some idea of what this object is supposed to look like when I get through. Whereas with whittling I just start cutting away pieces of wood 'til I see something taking shape and then I work toward that."

As I looked around his little workspace, I didn't see any carvings. "What do you usually whittle?" I asked.

The old man stopped his knife in mid-stroke and looked away as though he could see some of his old work in the Craven County sky overhead. Finally, he said, "When I was a little boy I used to make a lot of wooden knives. Seemed like every time I started whittling, the wood took on the shape of a knife. I guess that was because if you only cut away from you on a stick, after a while part of that stick's gonna get thinner and thinner. The thin part gets to be the blade and what isn't thin is the handle. Simple as that."

I asked him if he made anything other than knives.

"Oh, yeah," he said. "I make a lot of slingshots. Big ones, little ones. It's probably grandparents who get them for their grandchildren. I used to cut up old inner tubes to tie to the prongs of the stick until it got to where the fellow down at the garage started charging me for them. Now I just use the rubber bands that my daughter gets for me from her office. Now, don't you go telling anybody about that. Liable to get her in trouble."

The old man continued to cut on the small piece of wood he held in his hand. I noticed that he wasn't using a carving tool, just a regular pocketknife. "That must be a good knife to stay sharp enough to cut wood with," I said.

"It don't stay sharp, friend. I keep it sharp. There ain't nothing sorrier than a dull knife, no matter what you use it for. You get one that's got good steel in it and you can use it for a lifetime."

"You have that one for a long time?" I asked.

"About a week," he laughed. "I can't afford a good knife. A cheap knife cuts just as good as a high-priced one if you keep it sharp. Just wears out quicker."

I looked around the little shed and saw no evidence of any of his work. I said, "You must sell a lot of your work since I don't see any for sale."

He spit some tobacco juice over to the side of his bench as he continued cutting on the wood. "Don't never sell any. I give it all away."

"I'm sure there are lots of folks who would like to have some of your artwork and would pay you for it," I said.

"Probably so," he said. "Lady came by one time said she was from the arts council. Said she wanted to help me market my art. I told her I wasn't interested. I didn't have any art anyway, just some whittling. I'm going to give this thing, whatever it turns out to be, to that fellow at the garage. Maybe he'll swap it for an inner tube."

As I left the old man there at the produce stand, I thought there might be some things you can't put a price on.

The World According to Eli

E li used to sit on the porch there at Hinson's Store and talk to anybody who would listen. Sometimes, if nobody was there, he'd just talk to himself. Like a lot of old men, Eli was more than willing to share his experiences and the knowledge he had gained from those experiences.

One Saturday afternoon his only audience was J.C., Jake Lennon's youngest boy. It was one of those hot summer afternoons when there was no breeze and the shade of the porch offered very little respite from the heat. J.C. was sitting on the floor of the porch with his back against the wall of the store as far from the sun as he could get. Eli was sitting in the old rocking chair that he claimed as his. It really belonged to Mr. Hinson, but nobody except Eli ever sat in it.

"Age has a way of creeping up on you, boy," he said. "One day you think you can do anything, and the next day your mind is writing checks your body can't cash."

J.C. had no response to Eli's statement. He learned long ago that old folks didn't really care what he thought, and he knew that Eli would continue his solitary oration without encouragement.

There were rare occasions when Eli kept his thoughts to himself. In a way, he envied J.C.'s youth. J.C. was beginning a journey that Eli was about to complete. He felt compelled to give him advice, but he was constrained by experience. He had told Mr. Hinson the other day he had found that the best way to give advice to young folks was to find out what they wanted to do and then advise them to do it.

"You decided what you want to be when you grow up, J.C.?" he asked.

"Nope," was the solitary response.

"Well, you need to go ahead and do something. You can't sit around here the rest of your life waiting for life to come to you. Life ain't a spectator sport, you know. You gotta go down life's road like you know where you're going and experience everything you can. Along the way, when you're young, you're liable to get blamed for a lot of things you didn't do; then, when you get old, you'll get credit for things you didn't do, but you won't get either one if you never go down the road."

Eli's words hung in the heat of the afternoon. J.C. didn't answer, just looked out at the sun reflecting off the gas pump. He wondered what the old man had been like when he was younger. Did he make a lot of money? Had he seen a lot of places? Had he known any women?

"You ever been married, Mr. Eli?" he finally asked.

"I was married once. Once is enough if you do it right. She was a good woman. Probably better than I deserved. We lived together a long, long time. You know, boy, before a man and woman get married they can expect to live one lifetime each; then, when they get married, they got just one lifetime together. If you marry the right woman, that lifetime can seem real short; but if she ain't the right woman, it'll seem like a lifetime that goes on forever."

"How do you know if she's gonna be the right one?" the boy asked.

"Son, if I knew that answer I wouldn't be sitting on this porch. I'd be peddling that information to every man that walks and be the most admired man who ever lived."

Once again silence engulfed the two as they sat there on the porch of the store. The sun was just below the tops of the trees across the dirt road, and a few dark clouds could be seen on the horizon. One of those afternoon showers that come with every summer day would soon cool the air.

Eli thought about the boy sitting beside him. He had been a boy once with an uncertain future but with dreams and hopes. He wanted to tell the boy that life was his for the taking, but for all his philosophical utterances he couldn't think of just the right thing to say. Finally he said, "Boy, you live and learn, and then you die and forget it all."

✤ ✤ ✤

CHAPTER FIVE

southern ways

✤ ✤ ✤

Tobacco Days

The Border Belt Tobacco Market opened the other day. Even before I entered the warehouse where the sale was taking place, I heard the chant of the auctioneer. It was that serenade that first made me think about tobacco — not the plant itself but the way of life it created here in North Carolina and, subsequently, the effect its diminution has had on the people of this state.

The auctioneer's tune is often indecipherable to those who don't know what they are listening to. To the uninitiated listener, it is a series of words or just syllables with numbers interjected at apparently random intervals. The pitch of the auctioneer's voice can be perceived as either a musical sound or a whine. The perception, perhaps, depends on the price being quoted.

At the same time I heard the auctioneer, I could smell the tobacco. Anybody who has ever smelled it can quickly identify it when they smell it again. To those who appreciate tobacco, it's an aroma; to those who dislike it, it's a stench.

As I walked in the door of the warehouse, I saw sights similar in many ways to those I have seen for almost half a century. But, in many ways, it was different. There was still a queue of people following the auctioneer through the rows of tobacco, though not as many as in the past. It was a relatively quiet scene, quiet in comparison to the noise of crowds that once filled the warehouse at sale time.

The tobacco was still stacked in piles in rows that ran the length of the warehouse, but the stacks were different and the rows were shorter. Bales of tightly packed tobacco leaves had replaced the loosely tied burlap bundles, which had replaced the neatly stacked, circular piles of "tied hands" seen many years ago.

No folks from the stores or banks were there shaking hands with the farmers. There were no pretty girls serving lemonade — courtesy of the banks that had lent most of the farmers the money to raise and harvest the crop. Not many of the farmers had even shown up.

I walked over to the line of people who were following the auctioneer. I watched as the buyers occasionally stopped to pick out a leaf or two of the tobacco from a bale. They rubbed the leaf between their fingers, then dropped it and signaled the auctioneer to move along as they nodded their head to signal the bid. That gesture hadn't changed over the years.

Then I walked over and picked up a leaf of the cured tobacco. It was soft, smooth, and fragile. If I rubbed it too hard, the leaf would split but not crumble. I could wad it up, and it would spring back only slightly folded. I remembered that my grandmother, sitting in the pack house "grading" the tobacco, would have selected that particular leaf as a "wrapper," a leaf used to tie the bundle of leaves together at the top of the bundle.

I sat down on a small bale at the end of one row. It was so sturdy that my 200-pound bulk barely made a dent. I recalled the times my father had placed my sister and me on a pile of tobacco, given us a bag of boiled peanuts and a Coca-Cola, and left us in that heavenly circumstance while he watched the sale. Unlike the bale, that pile had been so soft it enveloped our small bodies.

So how about the taste of the tobacco? Well, I did actually wad up a leaf of tobacco one time and try to chew it. Suffice it to say that was not a good idea. But the taste of boiled peanuts still reminds me of tobacco auctions.

The poet Robert Browning probably would have understood my sensual reaction to the visit to the tobacco warehouse when he wrote:

> *How good is man's life, the mere living!*
> *How fit to employ all the heart and the soul*
> *and senses forever in joy!*

Tar Heel Born and Bred

F or all but the one year when I was exiled in Florida, I have always lived in North Carolina. Although I have traveled all over this country, I have always come back home. By choice.

What brought me back? Well, I could sentimentalize about the Carolina moon, Chapel Hill's intellectual climate, the girl I left behind, and Old Hay Street in Fayetteville, but all of those would be the incorrect answers.

What brought me back is the peculiar way North Carolinians have of accepting people and things for the way they are. Now that's not to say we don't take on airs every once in a while and talk about how "progressive" we are. We do that once in a while, particularly during elections. But most of the time we are "down home" as opposed to "up yonder" (Washington, D.C., or New York) or "out there" (Kansas or Oklahoma) or "way out there" (California).

We have never been known to be pretentious people. What you see is what you get. Some folks think that North Carolina, being a Southern state, is just like our neighbors Virginia and South Carolina — a little bit stuck up. But someone once correctly pointed out that North Carolina is "a vale of humility between two mountains of conceit."

Where but here, in the Land of the Long Leaf Pine, can you find a man in bib overalls, flannel shirt, and brogans driving a Mercedes to chase hogs back in the pen?

Where else can you find a college professor who refers to himself as "a good ol' beer-drinking redneck" who voted for Jessie Helms for the U.S. Senate and Bill Clinton for president?

Where else can you find a medical doctor who will chastise his patients for smoking the very tobacco that created the money to pay the doctor to tell the patient to quit smoking?

Where else could you find a power company that would build a nuclear power plant that cost several billion dollars (and still climbing) so it could save money?

Where else but in the Old North State could a former television commentator like Senator Helms get away with calling television news biased?

Where else could you get a hamburger steak with french fries and black-eyed peas served by a waiter in a tuxedo while you're sitting in a high-backed wicker chair at a table covered with a linen tablecloth?

Where else would people stand under a tree and argue for an hour about whether they are eating pe-*cons* or pe-*cans.*

Why would a state where almost every other person is a Baptist or a Methodist have a state bird named after an ecclesiastical official of the Catholic church?

Where else would you see ladies wearing ball gowns arrive at the country club in the same pickup truck their husbands went coon hunting in the night before?

Who else but a real Tar Heel would leave his beautiful home in the cool summer mountains to spend a week on a hot sandy beach while his brother leaves the warm coastal area to go snow skiing in the frigid air of those same mountains in the winter?

Where else would you find a town bold enough to be the home of the Bald-Headed Men of America and also host the state hairstyling competition? (That's Morehead City.)

Why would anybody leave here, go to Florida where the sun shines every day and palm trees shade the doorstep, but return to this place of contradictions?

Because North Carolina is home, and I love it.

Hard Times

I have been hearing a lot recently about the return of moonshining to the mountains. (As a matter of clarification for those who, through some grievous omission in their education, don't know what moonshine is, it is an illegal distillate made from corn and usually has a "proof," or percentage of alcohol, that far exceeds that of legal brew.) There is some question as to its absence in the first place, but, in any case, authorities say folks have gone back to making white lightning because of hard economic times in agriculture. This seems like a logical step for farmers who have a lot of corn on their hands and must otherwise rely on the market price they receive for their crops.

In trying to justify the resurgence of moonshining, I can't help but consider the unprecedented popularity of stock-car racing. It is fairly well known that stock-car racing got its impetus from the development of cars used to haul moonshine down dark Southern roads in a usually successful attempt to escape the law. It would make the cycle complete if some of these cars now running on the big tracks at Talladega, Charlotte, Rockingham, and others were to be used to assist in the marketing of this modern moonshining industry. It seems unlikely, of course. I can't see Jeff Gordon running moonshine.

Over the years people have been creative in coming up with ways to put food on the table when their usual source of income fails them. During the Great Depression, for example, some normally honest men took questionable measures just to make a few cents.

There was a man in Brunswick County who used mules to pull bogged automobiles through the swampy areas of the road by his house. To ensure a need for his services, each night he would haul barrels of water from Lockwood's Folly to the natural low places in the road. I'm sure some of his customers wondered why dust rose on each side of the mudhole, but they were in no position to question it.

Exhibition of wildlife used to be popular, too, particularly along the highways where tourists would travel. A frequent sight would be a bear caged behind a service station. Sometimes it would cost as much as a quarter to see it, or sometimes it was just an inducement to get the motorist to stop there for gas and get a free look at the bear.

I have heard of folks who took the animal exhibition a step farther by exhibiting unusual animals. The authenticity of some of the animals was questionable. The world's smallest lion looked a lot like Aunt Ella's cat with a creative haircut, and you would have to wonder how a cow could have quadruplets with such differences in their sizes.

Hard times do make honest people do things they wouldn't normally do. But I wonder about the amateur standing of a man who came to my grandfather's store many years ago. He had a bag full of items that he assured everyone was worth more than the requested price. I remember my grandfather listening to the peddler's spiel politely until the man brought out a set of false teeth, which he said was crafted by an artisan in Toledo, Spain. He further assured my grandfather that if he bought those teeth, he would have no problem speaking fluent Spanish. The salesman's credibility went right out the front door, followed by his suitcase.

Moonshiners don't have to worry about credibility. The product speaks for itself.

Climbing the Family Tree

G enealogy is usually thought of as an activity that provides for an accounting of our ancestors, a history of our family, or a tracing of our heritage. At least, that's the theoretical definition. In reality, there are some folks who take a different view.

Some people make up much of their heritage as they go along. It is always amazing to me to listen to some folks expound on their family history from one occasion to another. Here in North Carolina, it is not uncommon to find families whose Scottish heritage takes on the trappings of royalty, depicting every clan as directly descended from Bonnie Prince Charlie himself. Surely, there must have been more of the "common people" or else the prince was an extraordinarily busy and prepotent sire.

Other folks claim high-ranking descendants from various European families, African chieftains, and Asian princes. Ironically, these same folks say we should have stricter immigration laws.

Some folks get deadly serious about their ancestors. They search graveyards (cemeteries to polite folks) looking for names and dates that tell who begat whom and when they did it. Really kind of private stuff to be written down by and for people who might not even be family.

Genealogical searches, however, are usually done by a member of the family being researched. For some unexplained reason, that person is usually an unmarried female cousin or an aunt. It was in my family. Appropriately,

Cousin Helen was a librarian — someone not unaccustomed to looking through indices of names and familiar with the methodology of research.

These seekers of pedigree can be found in the Register of Deeds office, in the newspaper archives, and, more recently, on the internet. They are looking for anything that might shed some light on the family's past accomplishments and failures, some indication that we might have risen from poverty to prominence or fallen from distinction to anonymity. Of course, the real historian is the one who records everything, the good and the bad, without trying to make the history of the family something it isn't. Cousin Helen was a real historian who told the truth, good and bad.

There are many Cousin Helens throughout the South. They are usually the ones who instigate and organize family reunions. They are there at church homecomings and class reunions. Those are great occasions for gathering oral history — those stories of the saints and rascals who preceded us and, for better or worse, set the stage for the rest of us to follow.

Regardless of who the individuals were, everybody has interesting ancestors. They are interesting to the family, anyway. Some of us might look for the people who established the family as "prominent leaders in the community," while others might be more interested in finding out who were the wastrels and brigands, the colorful characters who are far more fascinating.

In any case, the pursuit of family history, while not limited to Southern families, is certainly of concern to almost every one in the region. And it's not just the high-society folks who are interested. The activity crosses every boundary of race, religion, and social strata. We all want to know who we were so we might be more likely to know who we are.

We can't choose our ancestors, and that's just as well. They probably wouldn't have chosen us anyway.

While we all are interested in where we came from, we should remember that the man who boasts only of his roots is conceding that he belongs to a family that's better dead than alive.

Color Lines

I first met Caleb when he was a little boy. His family sharecropped on my grandmother's farm. He was about my age, and he and I were playmates when we were really small; then we worked together on the farm as we got a little older. Although not many folks believe it today, back then I didn't think about his being of a different race. He was my friend.

When we were little, the two of us would ride double on the back of the mule that pulled the drag from the tobacco fields to the barn. When time came to grade and tie the tobacco, we would take turns pulling the dried leaves off the sticks and "making a hand" — bunching the individual leaves into a bundle that we handed to my grandmother.

It was an uncomplicated, childhood relationship that went along without much attention from anyone, including our families.

Last week I saw Caleb at a tobacco warehouse in Whiteville. In all honesty, I didn't recognize him; he recognized me. I'm sure he didn't recognize me because of any physical resemblance to my childhood appearance. In fact, he told me he only remembered me after he saw my name under the picture accompanying my column in the local paper. Both of us had changed a lot.

When he came up to me and introduced himself, I was naturally surprised. We had not seen each other in almost 40 years. We laughed about the changes in our appearance: the weight gain, the lack of hair (on his part), and the fact that both of us were now almost twice as tall as we were back then.

Then we talked about the other changes in our lives. We both had graduated from high school and gone on to college. That is where the similarities ended. Caleb had served in the Army during the Vietnam War. I had not. He graduated from college after he got out of the Army. He didn't talk about his time in Vietnam.

He did talk about his inability to find a job near home after he graduated from college. His degree is in business, but in the early 1970s he said, "there just weren't a lot of opportunities for black guys unless you wanted to use your race to take advantage of hiring quotas. I wanted to get a job based on my merit as an individual. I finally had to go to Baltimore to get a job where some of my family lived."

To his credit he did get a good job with a large corporation. He did well, advancing up the corporate ladder to a senior management position. He got married and has two children. Now he is retired and was back home for a visit and decided to go to a tobacco auction "just for old times' sake."

We talked about how much the tobacco business had changed. We laughed when we both noted almost simultaneously that there was nobody selling boiled peanuts in the warehouse. We talked about the bales of tobacco instead of the neat stacks of bundles and about the higher prices compared to what they were in the 1950s and 1960s.

Since there were no boiled peanuts readily available, we settled for a Pepsi and a pack of Nabs — just like we used to get working in the tobacco fields. Some of our tastes hadn't changed. While we ate, we continued to reminisce and bring each other up to date on our lives.

After we finished our snacks, we shook hands and said goodbye. On my way home I wondered, "Wouldn't it have been nice if Caleb could have stayed home and made a contribution to our community instead of Baltimore's?"

The Voice of Carolina

Sometimes when I'm a long way from home, someone will hear my Southern accent and ask me where I'm from. I used to be a little embarrassed to tell them I'm from a little rural community in southeastern North Carolina. After all, I had been off to college and traveled a good bit. I had even spent some time trying to get rid of my accent so that I could get a job doing radio and television commercials. I was never completely successful in eliminating my native brogue. Now I'm glad of it.

I did spend some time in the broadcasting business and did lose a little bit of my accent. Every once in a while one of my co-workers would point out to me what he considered a mispronunciation of a word, and I would change my way of saying that word for a little while.

But now I don't usually think about my accent. How I speak is a part of who I am. My accent is green tobacco gum and swamp mud. It's white rice and collards. It's mosquitoes and sweet potato pie. My accent is derived from a way of life that nurtured me and shaped me into whatever I am today.

When I was trying to get into the broadcasting business, I made an audition tape that the talent agency sent around to various advertising agencies. Weeks went by, and nobody called requesting my services. Finally, the agent asked one of the advertising guys what they didn't like about my voice.

"Oh, we like his voice fine. It's just like every other radio voice," he said. "They are a dime a dozen. We need voices that are distinctive."

So we went back and re-recorded that tape using my natural accent. I starting getting jobs. They were jobs advertising agricultural products or heavy equipment or similar items, but the pay was the same as the work for the banks and perfume companies.

"We like a Southern accent," said one New York advertising firm. "People feel like they can trust a Southern accent."

I trust a Southern accent, too. I don't mean the fake accents we hear on television but the real sound of the South that takes me back to the swamps and tobacco fields, to the cotton mills and country stores of my youth.

All the education in the world can't erase those sounds from my mind or eliminate them from my speech. I could live thousands of miles from here and still carry that sound of home with me.

I am no longer embarrassed by my Southern accent. I'm proud of it. It is a reflection of a place that is changing just like every other place in this country. We are more mobile now. We travel more frequently and hear more kinds of accents and languages. We hope our young people will grow up to be more educated, wealthier — and stay home. But they don't. They leave home, taking with them, just as I did, a part of all they have experienced.

When I write these stories, I hear those accents. I hear the farmhands, the old men eating their noon meal from small lard-tins brought from home to the sawmill, the men and women gathered in the churchyard after the Sunday morning sermon, and the young men at the garage talking about stock-car racing.

I hear the sound of their voices, their Southern accents ringing through my mind. They sound a lot like me.

Rules to Live By

I t is with some sadness that I note the passing of what had come to be known as "civility." I don't mean the social graces like table manners and that sort of thing. I mean the social actions and interactions we exhibit as we deal with each other.

In all honesty, "manners," the social graces, are a reflection of our attitude toward humankind. Civility is the attitude itself.

Growing up as I did in a small town in the rural South, there were certain things I was taught about how to deal with people. Most of the guidelines had some basis in the Scriptures we all learned in Sunday school. I expect that's where my parents got their guidelines and where their parents got theirs, and if it wasn't gospel when they got it, it became gospel by the time they told me about it.

Of course, there's the Ten Commandments right off the bat. There are all your basic guidelines right there handed down by God to Moses, who will forever look like Charlton Heston to me. (I know I should say I remember a particular Sunday school teacher or a preacher who made me remember the commandments, but it was really Charlton Heston who sticks in my mind. I guess he could have been a teacher or a preacher, but he chose to be an actor whose portrayal of Moses taught me more than most Sunday school teachers.)

Anyway, after you get past some of the strict "thou shalt not's," such as

"Thou shalt not kill," it all boils down to treating everybody with the respect that you expect them to show you. That's where civility has gone out the back door.

I always thought that if you met a funeral procession coming toward you on the highway, the respectful thing to do was to pull over to the side until it passed. That is a sign of respect for the family of the deceased. I don't see that much anymore. A Yankee friend of mine said that was a "Southern thing."

I also thought that children should never "talk back" to their parents, especially in public. I heard a lady in the grocery store the other day tell her adolescent son to push the shopping cart for her. With a bunch of other folks standing within earshot, he told her the cart was too full for him to push; she'd have to push it herself. If I had said something like that to my mother when I was that age (or any age), as soon as I could have picked myself up off the floor, my mama would have further publicly humiliated me right there in front of all those people by giving me a proper spanking.

Despite growing up with some rough-and-tumble characters in the log-woods and sawmills, as well as listening to the raucous and sometimes extremely colorful language of men plowing mules, I rarely, if ever, heard a man use foul language in front of a lady. Now, not only do I hear men talking like that with ladies present, I often hear the ladies using the same language or worse.

There is a Southern phrase of instruction my mother used to use when my sister and I would leave the house. After restating the time we were to be home, she would always say, "Y'all be sweet now, ya hear." That phrase is the greatest instruction for civility ever uttered. It encompasses all the Ten Commandments and probably every statute in every law book ever written.

Given that the Ten Commandments cannot be posted in a public building anymore, I think it would be extremely meaningful to have that most-civil approbation written over the door of every courthouse: "To all those who enter here, y'all be sweet now, ya hear."

~ ~ ~

CHAPTER SIX

music of life

King of the Road

As I look back on the more than half-century of my life, I can honestly say that the events in my life — from the most important to the least significant — have been connected with music. Almost every job I have had was musically connected. Most of the people I know, I met in some way through music.

So it was not unrealistic for me to think about different musical lyrics and tunes as I drove across the state the other day.

When my children were little, every family trip included a game that involved someone singing a song and another person shouting out the composer or, in the case of Broadway songs, the musical in which the song was sung. Not everyone always participated; my daughter and I were usually the only ones who enjoyed the game. My son would listen to his Walkman, and my wife would read a book.

But the other day as I drove alone, I began to look at my surroundings and tried to think of a song to match them.

I started out from Wilmington singing, "By the sea, by the sea, by the beautiful sea. You and me, you and me, oh how happy we'll be."

As I crossed the Cape Fear River it was, "Ol' Man River, that Ol' Man River, he must know somethin' but don't say nothin' …"

When I got out into the countryside and saw the acres of cotton, I thought of the folk song that spoke of "them old cotton fields back home."

The pine forests reminded me of one of my favorite songs from the musical *Paint Your Wagon*: "I talk to the trees but they don't listen to me. I talk to the stars but they never hear me."

All of those songs and the beautiful day made me nostalgic for those times when my mind could be occupied with such simple associations. I'm sure people in days past faced many of the same problems we face today: a need for more money, troubled personal relationships, and dissatisfaction with their jobs. But we could shake off the despair by singing "Oh, I got plenty o' nuttin'/An' nuttin's plenty for me." That's from *Porgy and Bess*, of course.

I saw a wide variety of houses as I traveled that day — brick houses, frame houses, mobile homes — all places where people lived. I thought about the people who lived in those houses, what they were doing, what kind of work they did, how many people lived there. I wondered how many were satisfied with their dwelling, how many were grateful for their homes. "Bless this house, oh Lord, we pray. Make it safe by night and day."

"Come to the church by the wildwood, Oh come to the church in the vale, No spot is so dear to my childhood, As the little brown church in the vale." I am always amazed at the number of churches I see as I drive through the state. There must be an awful lot of small congregations to need so many small churches in every community.

All those songs that we sang! They lifted our spirits, challenged our imaginations, and gave us all a common bond. I don't get to have the little musical contests anymore. On those rare occasions when I do have company with me on my road trips, I'm a little embarrassed to suggest such an activity.

But the songs are still there along the highways. The tunes and the lyrics are just "blowin' in the wind."

The Family with No Name

I t was in the late summer or early fall of 1958, and I was 15 years old. Mama had taken me to town to get my school clothes. The tobacco market was in full swing and other mothers and their children were doing the same thing we were. You could actually smell the tobacco in the warehouses, even downtown. The banks were busy cashing tobacco checks. Tobacco money paid for the clothes we bought and the car we rode in on.

Hulls from boiled peanuts littered the sidewalks and vendors were on every corner. "Get your boiled peanuts! Ten cents a bag!" And while they were selling peanuts for a dime on one corner, on another corner I saw a small family selling music. It was music without a price.

It was typical hot, steamy weather, and I could see the sweat-soaked shirt of the man playing the guitar. He had on a pair of denim overalls and a felt hat that he probably could have done without in that heat (the hat, not the overalls).

They were standing on the corner right across from where the Woolworth's was, and the two little girls, about five or six years old, kept looking at the people coming out of the store with packages. The girls looked and kept on singing.

The woman, apparently the mother, was the lead singer, and she played a Dobro stretched out perpendicular just above her waist. I thought it was a weird-looking instrument with an unusual sound. She had a pretty voice, if a little bit nasal, and the father sang a kind of high-pitched tenor harmony while the children sang along. It was old-time gospel songs they were singing. "In the sweet by and by, we shall meet on that beautiful shore ..." and "I'll fly away, Oh Glory, I'll fly away ..." They sang with fervor and from memory.

There were three boys in the group. The oldest was about my age. The middle son was about 10 or 12, and the youngest was about five or six. While the others sang, the youngest stood behind an upturned potato basket that had a stack of pamphlets on top of it. With one hand he offered the little brochures to passersby and with the other he held out a cigar box. I'm sure it was pride that made them sell the pamphlets instead of asking for a donation.

We went down the street to Manns Department Store and got my clothes. When we came out, the group was still singing in the hot afternoon sun. As we walked by, Mama bought a pamphlet. I couldn't tell how much was in the cigar box, but there was still a pretty good pile of pamphlets on the potato basket.

I asked Mama if she knew them and she said she didn't. Since Mama's world was pretty much my world, that made the little group a family with no name as far as I was concerned.

As we walked back to the car, I clutched my newly bought clothes and listened to the music of the family band. I had heard that kind of music on the radio. Every Sunday morning we used to listen to WENC, the local AM station, as local groups sang and a preacher preached. I wondered if that family had ever sung on the radio. I thought they were pretty good and envied the glamorous, show-business life I imagined they led.

Recently, I walked down that same street to that same street corner and for some reason the memory of that family came back to me as though it were yesterday. I could see the faces of each family member. And I could hear the music of the family with no name.

Maybe it was the heat. It still gets hot here. There were no peanut vendors, no crowded street, no dime store. And there will be just the remnant of the old tobacco market when it opens in a few weeks. But the music was still there. It must have adhered itself to the sidewalks and the buildings. Or maybe it had been hanging there in the air all these years. Maybe it needed my memory to set it free.

The Music Man

When I think of the people who have had an influence on my life, Paul Yoder immediately comes to mind.

In the years that I knew him I never called him by his first name. He was always Dr. Yoder. He was the chairman of the music department at Campbell College (now Campbell University) when I was a student there. In fact, my freshman year was his first year at Campbell as well. He was not what I had expected a music professor to look like. He was a big man, standing more than six feet tall and with a tendency to be "a little heavy." When he walked, he appeared to plod. He took big steps, his feet landing at a 45-degree angle from his body. His hair had begun to thin, and he combed it straight back. Because of its wispy nature, it never seemed to stay in place very long.

I had been on the Buies Creek campus a few days when I read a notice on the bulletin board notifying students who wanted to join the Campbell Choir to come by Dr. Yoder's office for auditions. I liked to sing, so I went to the music building (a connected group of old Army barracks) and into Dr. Yoder's office. Sitting at an old upright piano, he greeted me as I opened the door.

After I told him I wanted to audition for the choir, he got out an old hymnbook and told me to sing "Amazing Grace" as he accompanied me. After that he told me to sing the tenor line as he played. Then he picked out a song I had never heard, and he asked me to sing it. I couldn't read music so I asked him to play it through one time. He did and I sang it back to him just like he played it. He laughed and told me to report to the choir room the next day. I was to be a part of the Campbell College Touring Choir.

For the next four years I sang with that group. I learned a lot about choral music, how to sing, and how to create music. I even thought at one time I would become a music major, but after a short tenure in music theory class, Dr. Yoder convinced me I needed to consider another vocational endeavor. But he kept me in the Touring Choir. I was sometimes the only non-music major in the group, and those people in that choir became some of my closest friends.

I think back on Dr. Yoder now because he gave a very naïve, untutored, inexperienced country boy from Hallsboro the opportunity to experience music and travel that he never would have had otherwise. More important, he allowed me to become part of a group that gave me a sense of self-worth I didn't have, a sense of accomplishment that came from being in such a group and being recognized by other people as being part of that group.

Although he was always supportive, he was very frank in dealing with me. If I did not perform up to my potential, he would tell me in no uncertain terms that I "stunk," and my grade in that particular area would reflect his opinion. But he never let me quit. At one point I became so frustrated that I went into his office to resign from the choir. He told me to go ahead but if I did to never speak to him again. I stayed.

Even after I graduated, Dr. Yoder and I stayed in touch. For a period of time, I worked for Campbell University and saw Dr. Yoder almost every day. He became my friend and my counselor.

Every year, many young people leave the small towns of North Carolina and go on to institutions of higher learning. I'm sure many are just as dismayed as I was by the changes that take place in their lives when they leave the comfortable confines of family and familiar surroundings.

But I wonder how many are as fortunate as I was to have someone like Dr. Yoder to provide an anchor in the turbulent sea of academia. How many will find a mentor to guide them through the frustration of constant decision-making that is a part of the maturation process? I guess the inevitable question follows: "Are there any more like him around?"

The answer is yes. There are still teachers who care about their students even as the pressures of "bureaucratic education" close around them. They are there. They will make their presence known to those who need them. I hope those students will seek them out.

Southern Nights

B ack in the 1970s Glen Campbell recorded a song entitled "Southern Nights." I remember the song for two reasons.

The first reason has to do with my performance of that song as part of the Beaufort, South Carolina, Water Festival in 1977, I believe. I was the emcee for the festival beauty pageant, which was held on an outdoor stage near the waterfront. I was to run down the middle aisle of the theater while singing "Southern Nights" as part of the opening of the show, then onto the ramp that had been built out from the stage. This was back in the days before cordless microphones, and the technical crew had supplied me with extra cord to accommodate the production. Although all went well at rehearsal, on the opening night of the performance there was not sufficient cord to reach from the back of the theater where the soundmen were set up to the end of the ramp — much less onto the stage. Therefore, when I burst down the aisle singing "Southern Nights" at the top of my lungs, I was brought to a screeching halt — literally — just as I started to jump up onto the ramp.

I was not badly hurt, at least not physically. My pride, encased as it was in an entertainer's ego, was much more damaged. It is hard to salvage an image of self-assurance and confidence as one lies crumpled among the seats while gazing at the startled visage of a gentleman, his John Deere cap askew, trying not to lose the wad of chewing tobacco in his mouth.

I recall that night each time I hear "Southern Nights" on the radio. Fortunately, there are the other Southern nights that wash away at least part of that ignominy.

Which is the second reason I remember the song. It makes me think of those Southern summer nights I like so much. Some of those summer nights are out at baseball fields in the small towns that dot the North Carolina landscape. The lights illuminating the field can be seen for miles above the tops of the pine trees.

Sometimes the lights silhouette the town water tower or a church steeple as you approach the field where mothers and fathers, grand-mothers and grandfathers, and other assorted kin have gathered to watch the youngest pride of the family hit a ball off a pedestal or the somewhat-older offspring hit an inside-the-park home run.

Sometimes those baseball games are in stadiums where the more accomplished players comport themselves to the applause of the crowd while the smell of hot dogs and popcorn fills the night air.

Other summer nights in the South are filled with the smell of food cook-ing on a grill and the splash of youthful water sprites playing in backyard pools, rivers, or lakes as the sun casts its purple glow in the west — all mixed with the laughter of folks who enjoy being together.

But perhaps the best picture of summer nights in the South is much more tranquil. In this picture the affable socialization is replaced with quiet reflection as we sit in our backyard, on the porch, or on the more modern deck and watch the fireflies blink across the yard. Maybe there's the slow and amiable conversation between husband and wife as they share the secrets of how they got their flowers to look so fresh despite the daytime heat and how they have slowed the takeover of kudzu. Or they may relate the latest antics of the grandchildren. Or they may just sit there quietly sharing the pleasure of the other's company.

Those are the Southern nights I want to remember, the images I want to replace the memory of my embarrassment in Beaufort.

Two for the Show

A couple of months ago I was up in Tyrrell County to give a little talk to a civic club up there. I got there a little early because I didn't really know where the meeting place was, so I drove to downtown Columbia. The only resemblance between that Columbia and the one in South Carolina is the name.

Columbia is a beautiful little town right beside the Scuppernong River before it flows into Albemarle Sound. In the course of looking for the meeting place, I drove down to the end of a street, down to the river. It was "dusk dark," and the clear night sky held a full moon that reflected on the calm river water. The downtown businesses had closed except for a few cafés, and the streetlights gave the whole scene a look like a painting.

It was so quiet I could hear the water lapping against the dock at the end of the street. Then I heard a soft, rhythmic sound. As I looked in the direction of the sound, I saw two small boys sitting on a bench near the dock. One of them had two sticks and was beating out a rhythm on the back of the bench. I watched them for a few minutes; then the boy with the sticks gave them to his companion, who proceeded to produce his own rhythmic composition.

The first boy then began to beat a counter rhythm with his hands on the back of the bench. They alternated leads. The sticks would rest while the other's hands would continue; then they would swap before coming back together.

I was amazed at their spontaneous virtuosity. Two boys, no older than 12, playing on a river dock at dusk. They never even spoke to each other, as they seemed to be too caught up in their music to talk.

I was tempted to do my usual intrusive questioning of them. What were they doing there? Did they play like that often? But I didn't do that. I didn't want to break the spell.

Remembering I still didn't know the location of my speaking engagement, I reluctantly left the boys to their music. After driving to a convenience store and asking the clerk for directions to my destination, I followed his instruction and arrived just in time to speak.

After the meeting I asked my host about the two boys I had seen on the docks.

"Oh, yeah," he said. "That would be the Morton boys. You see them down there pretty often. Sometimes they'll get to doing a little improvisational dancing, too. You'd never know they were both mute. Some kind of birth defect."

That explained why they didn't talk to each other during the performance I saw. But I thought, "Those boys may not be able to speak, but they know how to communicate."

In further conversation with my host, I learned that the boys' father was a musician with a band that traveled around the country. Their mother worked at one of the cafés downtown.

As I drove back home that night, I kept thinking about those boys. Some might think they were disabled, but I didn't see them as disabled. I saw them as two gifted young men who knew how to make music in a silent world.

❦ ❦ ❦

CHAPTER SEVEN

rhythm of the seasons

❦ ❦ ❦

Always in Autumn

A s I write this, the weather has taken a decidedly cooler turn. This is good news since the hot weather of the summer has taken its toll on me.

But beyond the obvious relief from the heat, the change to autumn-type weather reminds me of all those years when school was the focus of my life. By school I mean from the first grade through college.

Starting school meant getting new clothes, new books, and new teachers, as well as meeting a few new students. In the small rural schools such as Hallsboro, there were not that many new students. For almost all of the 12 years I went to school there, I saw the same faces every year. Usually, when the occasional new face showed up, it was only temporary. They moved on before the year was over.

But when I went off to college, fall took on a whole new meaning. For one thing, almost every face I saw was new. My clothes were not always new, but they were good enough to serve the purpose. The people who sat beside me in class, walked across the campus with me, ate meals with me, and generally shared the anxiety of college life were not too concerned about what I wore.

Starting school every year created excitement because I didn't know exactly what lay ahead. During grade school and high school, there was a mixture of social eagerness combined with the knowledge that my life was changing and rushing toward a time when the familiarity of friends and teachers would no longer be there. I had to face the fact that sooner rather than later I would be on my own. When that time came, I looked around that college campus and realized that home was a long way from there. I knew things would never be the same again.

I went through an annual assessment of my life every fall for almost 18 years. Then one fall came, and there was no school to go to. I saw school buses going down the road and students driving to school, and I realized that for the first time none of that would be in my life. It was a shock.

After the shock wore off, nostalgia set in. I pictured in my mind the bright foliage that covered the college campus in the fall, the slight tension of the first class meeting in a subject I didn't particularly want to take, the smell and feel of new books, the euphoria of the cold wind blowing across the football stadium on a Saturday afternoon, the late-night gatherings at the little café down the street, the bull sessions and the "intellectual" discussions, the excitement and dread of waiting for grades to be posted, and Grandmama's cookies from home.

Then reality took over. The rent was due, the car payment was due, and the house was cold. Christmas was coming, and my small paycheck meant minimal gifts for everybody. This is what I had gone to school for all those years?

Then came the babies and better jobs, and life began to improve generally. But my life still ran on the school year. It seems that every significant fact of my life has taken place in the fall. I was born in the fall, started school in the fall, finally got out of school in the fall, got married in the fall (both times), every job change has come in the fall, and I'll bet when I die it will be in the fall.

The third season has given inspiration to poets for centuries. It has even inspired some good ol' boys like me from Columbus County.

> *Autumn rests softly on our memories,*
> *And golden days and blue-lit nights sprinkle stardust*
> *In a thousand different eyes.*

Christmas Spirits

I f shopping mall activity is any indication, Christmas is a dichotomy. Before December 25, people are nice. On December 26 the Spirit of Christmas is replaced by demons that possess every person who ventures out of the house and into the malls. Normal civility is replaced by an aggressiveness that would make Attila the Hun run for the hills.

"What do you mean, 'All sales are final'?"

"Look at this, Mabel. My Melvin paid 250 bucks for this coat. Now it's on sale for $29.95! He is so stupid!"

"What do you mean my credit card is rejected? My wife is the only one to use it and there was a $5,000 limit on it!"

"I don't care if my size is a 32B. The 36C is on sale and I'm buying it!"

Before Christmas the mall was crowded, but people would let you pass. On December 26 people walk resolutely in a straight line like Dirty Harry on the trail of the bad guys. No one yields the right of way, if such a right of way existed. The mall shopper's eyes are focused somewhere way down the mall. If someone steps from a store without looking both ways, they get run over.

Kids on skateboards have decided that it is too cold outside to experiment with their new Christmas gifts, so they line up and race down the mall scattering even the Dirty Harrys as the boards weave in and out of the walking traffic. There are the usual mall walkers who come in for their exercise. Today they are not walking. They are jogging, even running, to get out of the way.

Each little seating oasis is occupied by men, most of them wearing new Christmas-gift jackets with matching sneakers. Some are sleeping. Some are sitting upright, eyes unblinking like zombies. They wait there until their female companions come to give them the command to move out.

The mountain of manmade snow where Santa and his elves reigned just two days before now stands abandoned, awaiting the demolition crew that will dismantle and cart away the last vestige of the Yuletide goodwill that once emanated from the display.

But the dichotomy is not so evident in the small towns that cover North Carolina. In the family-owned stores where the shopper and the owner probably went to school together, there is a different feeling.

As the shoppers come into the store they are greeted with, "Hey, Joe. Y'all have a nice Christmas?"

"We sure did. Most of the children got home, and I ate so much I'm probably going to fast for the rest of the week. Listen, Mama gave me this shirt and it's about two sizes too small. I guess she thinks I'm still her little boy. You got anything I can exchange it for?"

"Sure. Just pick out something about the same price and I'll put this back in stock. ...Thanks for coming in, Joe. Tell your mama and them I said "Happy New Year" now, ya hear."

The two scenes may be a slight exaggeration, but not much. In the small towns the salespeople and the customers will see each other all year. They'll greet each other after church on Sunday and sit together at the high school ball games. They'll eat together at the Rotary Club on Thursday nights and raise money for the volunteer fire department on Saturday.

The people who come into the stores in the small towns aren't just customers. They're friends. And that keeps the demons from chasing away the Christmas spirit.

The Day After

Now that Christmas is over and the New Year is upon us, what do we see? Considering all we ate over the holidays, it is probably not our toes.

One of the treasured traditions of Christmas is feasting. So much of what we do during the holiday season has to do with eating: church socials, parties, family gatherings, and more. No wonder Santa Claus is a bit overweight.

The food we eat at Christmas is not conducive to dieting. I have no idea how many calories there are in fruitcake or those little chocolate-covered peanut-butter balls or pumpkin pie or turkey dressing or even butter-basted turkey for that matter. I believe I can safely assume that the total amount of calories (or fat grams or whatever it is that adds weight to my body) consumed during Christmas should be enough to last me about a year if I could go and hibernate like a bear.

Unfortunately, I can't hibernate. That doesn't mean that my lack of physical activity could not be mistaken for hibernation. Hibernation means "to pass the winter in a torpid or resting state." Other words that come to mind are "sluggish," "dormant," "numb," "apathetic," and the dominant phrase "lazy."

Certainly the casual observer could mistake my lack of mobility for the comparable comportment of a bruin ensconced in his winter cave. After a filling holiday repast I do tend to recline in a supine position, close my eyes, and let all that gastronomic intake turn to fat.

And, as with the hibernating bear, it is not wise to disturb my slumber.

Such a move on the part of family or friends can arouse a wrath not usually seen in my typically amiable state.

Excessive food consumption and the availability of the reclining chair have to be one of the most sleep-inducing combinations ever conceived. I feel sure that if the aforementioned bear had access to a recliner he would stay in his cave year-round. Needless to say, this could lead to a decrease in bear population since at least some waking time has to be allotted to repopulating the species.

The likelihood, however, of prolonged inertia is annulled by the ever-present and obligatory "chores." This category of labor is divided into two major subsections: (1) holiday-related chores and (2) regular, everyday chores.

Holiday chores include taking down the Christmas tree. At my house this task is mandated by the woman of the house to be completed no later than midnight on December 26. Failure to complete said task in the allotted time can result in expulsion from the dwelling and/or an intolerable silence that lasts until the task is completed.

It is a fairly simple job to remove the ornaments from the tree, wrap them individually in tissue paper, and place them in a box to be so positioned in a closet that its retrieval next Christmas will involve the complete evacuation of that space. The really tough job is removing the lights from the tree. Once upon a time, Christmas lights were red, white, blue, and green and were each about the size of my thumb. Our current Christmas tree lights are all white, very small, and number in the thousands. Removing them from the tree is a major operation demanding tremendous concentration and the dexterity of a surgeon. Of course, no matter how hard I try, the majority of the lights will not be fit for use next year — necessitating the purchase of another thousand or so.

Other holiday tasks include disassembling all the other decorations that have graced the house since the beginning of the season. Since the removal of the tree and its decorations usually puts me in a mood to destroy everything else in my path, removal of said decorations doesn't take long. The same can be said of the other everyday chores. If it isn't nailed down, sealed to the house, or otherwise secured, it is thrown away with a lack of restraint reminiscent of Genghis Khan sweeping across the steppes.

Of course, once I have accomplished my appointed chores, I return to my pseudo-hibernation to issue in the New Year.

Winter of My Discontent

I have said on many occasions that I don't like cold weather. That is a truism that will hold for eternity. I do enjoy, however, two things associated
with cold weather: burning leaves and chopping wood.

I love the smell of leaves burning, the warmth of the fire as the cool fall air
whips around me. I like to sit by the burning pile as dusk settles and stare into
the embers, watching them fade into ashes.

I like to feel the ax split the wood, to hear the solid thud as the two pieces
fall to the side, to smell the wood as it opens itself to the brisk air, and even to
feel the contentment that comes with resting after the physical exertion.

I don't enjoy the processes that lead to those activities: raking leaves and
cutting up trees.

That is what is referred to as an irresolvable dilemma or being between
a rock and a hard place. The only resolution is to have somebody else do
the prerequisite labor. That usually involves coercing or paying somebody.
And therein lies the rub. I don't enjoy burning leaves and chopping wood
enough to pay somebody to create the necessary circumstances and, since
my son is no longer at home, I can't force anybody else to do it.

So it falls to me to do my own dirty work. Anybody who has a yard full
of pecan trees does not lack for leaves. Back during the fall, I was able to
take advantage of the use of a lawn sweeper to get the leaves up and piled
in an area where they could be burned. Recent winter storms have created

enough fallen tree limbs to supply me with enough wood to last for as long as I will be able to cut it.

Alas, all is not ready for the good part. If you remember, this fall was so dry that burning leaves could have set off a wildfire that would have swept over the area and made Sherman's bonfire in Atlanta look like a weenie roast. So I didn't burn any leaves. I just piled them up and waited for a more appropriate time to burn them.

Then came the rain. Have you ever tried to burn pecan leaves that have been drenched by rain and allowed to soak until the pile is so sodden that a blowtorch would only create steam? Did you know that a pitchfork handle will snap under the weight of a single load of wet pecan leaves? That giant pile of leaves is too heavy to move without a bulldozer and too wet to burn, so it will just have to stay there until the sheer weight of the pile causes it to sink into the depths of the earth where it will, undoubtedly, fuel Hell for eternity.

I said something about the limbs falling and providing the wood that I would split to go in my fireplace. There were, indeed, plenty of fallen limbs as a result of the ice storm. I do, indeed, want that wood in my fireplace. I would, however, rather cut it up first. Unfortunately, I was deprived of that exercise this year as one limb from an ancient tree not only fell from the tree onto my house but also, like a wooden Santa, came down my chimney.

My wife was the first to discover the pecan limb in our fireplace. Just having the wood arrive in that manner would have been cause enough for alarm and dismay, but to find the detritus of a year's worth of accumulated chimney matter, particularly soot, scattered across her white carpet caused her to shriek as if all of her fingernails were being cut short and painted black.

So this year, instead of bringing in firewood from outside and putting it in the fireplace, I am taking wood out of my fireplace and putting it outside.

So much for the romance of cold weather.

My Valentine

As I write this, Valentine's Day is approaching. Probably by the time you read this, you will have either received or given a Valentine gift from/to someone you love. Or at least think you love. Or maybe hope you will love in the future. I'm still trying to think of something unique to do for my wife on this Valentine's Day so I thought I'd jot down some thoughts about the subject.

Valentine's Day is a once-a-year thing. Real love is more permanent.

I assure you I am not an expert on love, because love is different for everybody. Poets and songwriters have been trying for years to tell us about love and how it works. Although they have made valiant and beautiful efforts, they have just touched the surface.

After some thought on the subject, I have come up with a few conclusions based on my own often-woeful experience, as well as some observations of people who are really in love.

Love is sitting up all night in a hospital waiting room by yourself. This covers waiting for a baby (or babies) to be born, as well as those less pleasant reasons.

Love is watching her sleep. She doesn't have her makeup on or her hair brushed, and those wrinkles are a little more obvious. But somehow she still looks like the young girl you married.

Love is the feeling you get watching your son get his first haircut.

Love is bringing her flowers when it's not a special occasion. Special occasions (like Valentine's Day) take all the spontaneity out of gift giving. The special look to match the occasion is her reaction to the unexpected. It'll also make her wonder what you're up to.

Love is when you enjoy her beating you at Monopoly. When that happens, just hint that you let her win even if she beat you fair and square. Then run like crazy.

Love is when she fixes your favorite meal even when she is as tired as you are.

Love is the smell of baby powder. First of all, baby powder just smells good, but sometimes its greatest value is to replace the smell of dirty diapers. Real love is when you change the diapers.

Love is when she walks by your chair and just touches the top of your head. That little action indicates a familiarity that only the two of you share. And, as the song says, if everything goes well, "this could be the start of something big."

Love is wearing that pink shirt she bought for you. You haven't worn a pink shirt since the days when Elvis was your hero, but now you are her hero.

Love is watching a Lifetime Channel movie together. It's real love if you can watch two in a row.

Love is holding hands in the car while driving to the grocery store.

Love is making up your own poem for a Valentine card instead of buying one already written.

Love does not mean never having to say you're sorry. Love mean saying you're sorry and meaning it.

Love can be confusing. It can make you so sad you want to cry and so happy you want to fly at the same time. Love is one of those things you can't buy or catch or mount on your wall. Love is like money: No matter how much you have, you always want more.

And love can make you philosophical, when you have to stop and think about it.

Strawberries for Sale

It's strawberry season. By the time you read this, the North Carolina Strawberry Festival will have ended in Chadbourn for another year and the committee will already be working on next year's celebration. But just because the festival is over doesn't mean that you can't still buy strawberries.

The big auction market that existed many years ago in the Columbus County town is gone and in its place is a multitude of roadside operations where strawberry buyers can pick their own if so inclined, or they can buy them already picked and packaged. It was one of those stands that caught my eye the other day.

It really wasn't the stand itself that got my attention. It looked like so many others that we see — a pickup truck with a shelter built onto the back and a hand-lettered sign propped up against the side. Boxes of strawberries filled the bed of the truck.

What got my attention were the two purveyors of berries who staffed the stand. One was an older lady, her gray hair pinned up in an old-fashioned bun. She was wearing a pair of blue bib overalls, a white T-shirt advertising Myrtle Beach, and a pair of very worn tennis shoes. The aluminum lawn chair she had chosen as her sales station had sunk into the sandy soil, making the seat of the chair only about two inches above the ground. I guess she didn't mind that because she never got out of that seat anyway.

But her little companion moved around enough for both of them. The little girl looked to be about 10 years old. She was dressed comfortably in a pair of shorts, a T-shirt, and Air Jordans.

It was a school day, and I wondered why she wasn't in school instead of out by the roadside peddling strawberries. I stopped my car and went over to the stand. My wife had told me to buy some good strawberries if I found any, so I decided to see if those offerings met the criteria.

As I looked at the berries the little girl came over and said, "Them's good 'uns right there. Picked 'em myself this morning."

I smiled at her enthusiasm as she perched herself on the tailgate of the truck. "Go on and eat one if you want to. My grandma says they don't taste as good as they used to, but I like 'em. Don't nothin' taste good as it used to to Grandma."

She sat there on the tailgate swinging her little legs back and forth with an eagerness only youth can exhibit. I asked her how much the berries cost, and she told me. She immediately added, "That's a good price. You ain't goin' to find 'em that good in the grocery store. Grocery store berries ain't got much taste, to tell you the truth. Here, take one. Taste it."

She picked up a plump berry and handed it to me. "Just hold onto the green part there so you don't get the juice on your fingers," she instructed.

I took a bite of the fruit and it was, indeed, delicious.

"I believe I'll take a quart of these," I told her.

"Cheaper if you buy 'em by the flat," she said. "but that don't matter to you, I reckon."

"Now what makes you think that?" I asked.

She answered by saying, "Usually a man wearin' a shirt and tie ain't worried about money. Grandma says shirt and tie folks is paper shufflers. Y'all don't really have to work 'cause you get government money."

"That your grandmother over there?" I asked, indicating the lady in the lawn chair.

"Yep, that's her. She don't have to work neither," she said.

"Why not?" I asked.

"Because she's got me," was her reply.

I bought a flat.

Coming of Age

S eems like spring is the shortest season of the year. I know that just a few days ago the temperature was in the low 40s and the night frost had killed everybody's tomato plants. We had moved frost-threatened flowers in and out of the house so often the pots were getting worn out from the bottom.

Now, the weather is so warm that a leisurely stroll brings out the perspiration, the lakes and rivers are full of boaters, and pale sunbathers are already turning pink.

I couldn't help but notice how the quick transition of the season coincided with school graduations, both college and high school. Like the change in the season, there doesn't seem to be a very long transition period now for those graduates either. College graduates, particularly, will immediately have to change their everyday attire from baggy pants and sweatshirts to suits and ties.

But the biggest adaptation will have more to do with how they live than how they dress. The acceptance of responsibility for their everyday existence will be a challenge for some who have relied on their parents for rent money, automobile insurance, electricity bills, phone bills, and all the other costs of living. For some it will be a shock. For others it will just be one more step toward maturity. In either case, like the changing season, there is not much time to adjust.

This all comes to mind because my son will graduate from college this spring. Fortunately for him, this life-passage will be just another step toward adulthood. It took him a while to accept the inevitability of maturation, but he has done so and is moving on. And, like most fathers, I feel compelled to pass on a portion of my accumulated wisdom to him. So here it is.

Never forget who you are. Be proud of your heritage but don't be "prideful." We are the only ones who know that all our geese are swans.

Go to church every Sunday. Beyond all the benefits you will receive from attendance, it is something you are supposed to do as a member of this family and the family of God.

Get only one credit card. One is a necessity. Two is a temptation. More than two is a burden.

If you work for a man, give him a full day's work. He is paying you for a full day's work. If you give him less, you are stealing from him.

Have confidence in your abilities, but never be afraid to learn from other people. Everybody makes mistakes. Learn from yours and everybody else's as well.

Read at least one book a month. Never let television, movies, or the internet replace books.

Write letters. It is easier to use the telephone or the internet, but writing a letter is more personal. You can't see teardrops on email. Your handwriting is an extension of your mind and heart. Share it.

Set aside some time just for yourself. Never be so busy that you don't have time to stop and think about the real world around you.

Take in every drop of life. Don't sip it. Drink it down in great gulps. There is so much to do and see, so many people to meet and know, so many experiences to be a part of that you have to grasp every opportunity when it presents itself; then savor it later.

I'm sure my son won't take all that advice. But maybe he will learn it for himself during the lifelong maturation process.

The Sound and Fury

M ama always said there is some good in everybody and some good will always come from everything that happens. Hurricanes belie that belief.

Last week as I stood on the porch of my house and watched the wind blow the rain horizontally across my lawn, watched trees fall around the house, saw pieces of siding become disengaged from my dwelling, I thought about what Mama had said and for once found Mama wrong.

There is nothing good about not having any electricity. There are those who say we are spoiled, that we have gotten used to electricity and now rely on it too much. Our ancestors got along fine without it. That is probably true, but we are living in a time when electricity is a necessity and we are not prepared to do without it.

Not living in a municipality means relying on a pump in the yard for our water supply. The pump requires electricity. No electricity, no water. No water means no baths and no plumbing that works. Those two conditions alone can create not only physical discomfort for yourself but also for those around you. Under other circumstances where such conditions exist, you could go out in the woods and stay away from everybody else. Hurricanes eliminate that option.

Hurricanes occur during hot weather. Humidity is high. No electricity means no air conditioning. No fans. No sleep. The result of all that means there are some cranky folks forced to stay together in fairly close quarters for an extended length of time. Ergo, sometimes the fury of the hurricane raging outside is matched by the fury raging inside.

There is nothing good about cleaning up the mess created by a hurricane. The sight of fallen trees and other debris scattered across your property is sad. But the sad sight stirs a little bit of anger, too. Why does this happen? I do not want to get out that chainsaw again. I spent many years getting an education so that I would not have to do that kind of manual labor. Hurricanes have no respect for education.

It seems that there have been more hurricanes in recent years. I am one of those folks who used to measure every hurricane by Hazel. Hazel is now a diminished benchmark. You now hear: "This wasn't as bad as Fran." I personally didn't have as many trees to fall during Bonnie as I did during Fran. But that may not have anything to do with the fierceness of Bonnie or lack thereof. Fran had taken almost all the trees I had. There wasn't much left for Bonnie. I figure after a few more hurricanes I won't have to worry about cleanup. There will not be anything to destroy. It will all be gone.

I don't know why I fuss so much about hurricanes. There is nothing I can do to stop them from occurring. There is nothing I can do to keep them from damaging homes and property. There is nothing I can do to keep them from changing people's lives. In view of that inability to make a difference, I am reminded of a speech from Shakespeare's *Macbeth*:

> *She* (Hurricane Bonnie?) *should have died hereafter;*
> *There would have been a time for such a word.*
> *To-morrow and to-morrow, and to-morrow,*
> *Creeps in this petty pace from day to day,*
> *To the last syllable of recorded time;*
> *And all our yesterdays have lighted fools*
> *The way to dusty death. Out, out, brief candle!*
> *Life's but a walking shadow, a poor player*
> *That struts and frets his hour upon the stage,*
> *And then is heard no more; it is a tale*
> *Told by an idiot* (me?), *full of sound and fury,*
> *Signifying nothing.*

Maybe hurricanes really ain't no big thing.

Yard Duty

U sually when somebody reflects on the joys of summer, the subject includes the beach or the mountains or a baseball game or some other pleasant situation normally associated with the season. Unfortunately, I cannot follow that pattern.

You see, I am a captive of my lawn. I might as well be bound and tethered to one of the few remaining trees that still stand despite the efforts of a succession of hurricanes to blow them down. I cannot leave my lawn unattended for more than seven days for fear that I may lose sight of my house and therefore remain without lodging for the remainder of the hot weather still to come.

This is the first year in many that I have taken on the challenge of maintaining my lawn. In previous summers my business travel schedule didn't enable me the time to tend to the lawn properly so I used the services of a very competent lawn service. As my schedule was considerably changed this year, however, I figured I could do the necessary mowing and trimming and save a little money at the same time. That may still be the case, but it comes at a great price.

My lawn is a pretty good size, but it also has several planted impediments that make mowing it at least an eight-hour job. The house was built in 1854, and I truly believe that each tenant added some shrubbery, bush, or plant each year since then. Especially evident is the wisteria. When this vine is blooming, it has beautiful flowers. But it spends the rest of the time insinuating itself into the limbs of trees and shrubbery to the point that all other growth is stymied. You cannot slow its growth by cutting it off above ground. It must be pulled up by the roots, which can go on interminably through flowerbeds and across the lawn. Pulling up wisteria roots is not a job for the fainthearted, especially during hot weather. Gulping gallons of Gatorade is a negligible but necessary accompaniment for the exercise.

In all honesty, the pruning and pulling necessary to tend the plants and shrubs are secondary to the foremost task of mowing the grass. Not only must I navigate around the numerous aforementioned impediments, but I must also cut over anthills, dodge holes (lawn dents made by falling tree limbs courtesy of hurricanes), and concentrate on not getting run over by passing traffic.

Perhaps all of this could be considered a less stressful situation if I weren't required to do it so often. If I could mow the lawn, say, every two weeks that might even be enjoyable. But, alas, I must mount my trusty lawnmower and grab my weed trimmer at least once a week, and often twice a week if it rains. Sometimes when I sit on the deck at the back of the house, I can hear the grass growing. I can hear a squeaking sound as the just-cut leaves push themselves through the soil.

I was in the lawn and garden store the other day when the clerk asked if I needed any fertilizer for my lawn. The hapless lad probably didn't even know how close to death he came. Fertilizer I don't need. In truth, much of the grass in my backyard is aided and abetted by the septic tank line. Talk about natural fertilizer.

At the end of my eight-hour lawn maintenance, I can look back at the green carpet that surrounds my house, inhale the smell of freshly mowed grass, walk barefoot across the moist turf, and reflect on the beauty that has resulted from my labor.

Until the next week.

✿ ✿ ✿

CHAPTER EIGHT

----

just a thought

✿ ✿ ✿

Weird Stuff

In the course of an otherwise normal conversation, a lady asked me how I come up with the "weird" stuff I write about. I told her I honestly didn't know. Upon reflection and adequate time to come up with a better answer, I still don't know.

The question did cause me to look back at some of the topics I have written about during the 15 years — off and on — I have been writing columns and stories.

Several topics had to do with farm animals. I don't find this unusual in this part of the country, which is still primarily rural despite the subtle encroachment — and exit — of industry. Most of the folks I know are only one or two generations removed from the farm. In truth, however, for years the mule was my most frequent farm animal topic, and said animal is quickly becoming a less than conspicuous presence in North Carolina. One reason I give mules so much attention is because I hope they might make a comeback if more people know about them and the contributions they have made to the economy and social heritage of the state. I don't believe this is an unlikely possibility. If you remember, Republicans were almost extinct in North Carolina once. Now look at 'em.

Much of my writing has dealt with the way things used to be. Admittedly, the nostalgic look at our past may not be entirely objective since I can only look back at the things I have personally seen or heard.

Other folks' recollections are similarly influenced by their individual perspectives. Since the period of my lifetime has only passed (fairly recently) the half-century mark, I am limited by that timespan in recalling the circumstances that I can write about with some credibility. Therefore, I must rely on my alter ego, Eli, to talk about those things that preceded my lifetime.

Eli is a composite character made up of the impressions I have gotten from many of the older people I have known. He embodies the heritage of the people of this state; he is a man who believes in the virtues of hard work and in an honest day's work for an honest day's pay. He is conservative in his belief in God and the role He plays in the lives of human beings. He is a man tied in some way to the earth. Humor is an essential part of his view of life. Eli is "a Tar Heel born and a Tar Heel bred and when he dies he'll be a Tar Heel dead."

With so many newcomers moving here from out of state, I hope I can let them know a little about their new neighbors — past and present.

I have often used my writing to extol the virtues of the natural beauty of this state. That is something we all see every day and often take for granted. I hope I can capture a bit of the wonder it creates.

But I can't talk about the mountains or the sea or the farmland or the wildlife or the forest without talking about the people who affect and are affected by that beauty. That's why I write about the hermit in the Great Dismal Swamp, the deer hunters from Mount Gilead, the men at the sawmills in Pender County, the tobacco farmers and their families in Columbus County, the shad fishermen in Beaufort, the firefighters of the Forest Service, and the old man who tends a private graveyard in the Green Swamp.

I write about other people who also make North Carolina unique — the waitresses in the local cafés, the schoolteachers in the rural schools, the preachers in the small churches who preach because they are "called" even when there may not be much money to pay them, the men and women who run the crossroads stores, the doctor who still makes house calls, and the barber who shuns the title of "hairstylist."

I don't think that's such weird stuff to write about. Now, the occasional 'possum or goat story might qualify.

The Real Scoop

According to most folks, as we get older we are supposed to be less likely to believe everything we see or hear. This supposition has some basis in fact since many of us tend to have poorer eyesight and hearing as we get older, causing us to question our ability to differentiate between truth and fiction.

With this in mind, I am continually amazed at the number of people who buy and, supposedly, read the supermarket tabloids. Every time I go to the grocery store I see somebody buying one of those publications, yet when I ask folks if they saw a particular article in said publications, the answer is invariably "no."

I thought about this the other day in the supermarket when a publication in the rack got my attention. The headline read: "Robot Gives Birth to Human Baby." Now you have to admit that would get your attention, too. Although I knew that the credibility of such journals is only slightly lower than that of former President Clinton, my curiosity forced me to buy it.

Of course, once I read the story, it was not about a robot giving birth to a human baby at all. The real story was about the use of robots to provide household services. I didn't get the connection.

But as I read some of the other stories in that broadsheet, I wondered what other people think when they see those headlines as they wait to pay for their groceries. What would they think if they saw the headline (also in the issue with the robot) that read, "Gay Vampire Catches AIDS," as they paid for a loaf of bread and a gallon of milk?

One thought-grabber was "New Machine Sucks Pounds off Your Body." The image I saw was of a tiny vacuum cleaner cruising my body like a vigilante looking for street punks. I wondered how it could tell the fat from the parts of my body I wanted to keep.

I wondered about the parents of the twin brother and sister who had a mutual sex-change operation. Did they say, "Look at it this way: We may have lost a daughter but we gained a son ... and vice versa"?

The most intriguing headline was "Woman Attacked by Bees While Taking a Bath in Honey." That raised several questions. Where did she find that much honey? Think how long it took to fill the tub. How do you find the soap in a tub full of honey? What industrial-strength solvent did she use to clear the drain? As for the bees, two six-packs of Coors would have been a safer way to get a buzz.

There are always articles about celebrities in these rags. Since Princess Diana died, the writers have had to search for other grist for their mill. I must admit I did have some interest in the number and size of rings in Shania Twain's navel, but I really don't care if Frank Sinatra's ghost is haunting the streets of Las Vegas.

As I pondered the reasons why people continue to buy these journalistic rejects, I heard two ladies in the checkout line talking about a recent episode of "The Jerry Springer Show," which is the supermarket tabloid of television. He is one of the highest paid performers on the air. Since the two productions, one print and one video, are so profitable, the logical conclusion has to be that this is what people want.

That's as amazing as a robot giving birth to a human.

A Few Regrets

L ike most people, I sometimes look back on my life and wonder what I would change if I could go back and do it all over again. Every time I begin this reflection, I am reminded of the lyrics of a Frank Sinatra (Elvis Presley, Neil Diamond, and others) song that says, "Regrets? I've had a few, but then again, too few to mention." But I thought I'd mention them anyway.

I'd go to school longer before getting a job. Not only can you never learn enough or be too prepared, but as long as you stay in school, nobody expects much of you except to make grades that are good enough for you to stay in school.

I would never own or lease a car. Not only would it eliminate a monthly car payment and car insurance premiums, but I would always have an excuse for not being able to go to some event I didn't want to attend and I would never be asked to lend a car to somebody who would wreck it some night right after I made the last payment.

I would go to more musical concerts (in somebody else's car). I would listen to a wider range of musical styles, even hard rock. There must be some reason I have missed that allows that music to exist.

I would learn to draw and paint. I have always wanted to be able to capture on canvas not so much the scenes that I see every day but those scenes that exist only in my mind.

I would let my emotions be more evident. I would laugh more and cry more. I would be less tolerant of my own mediocre efforts in letting people know how I really feel when I'm angry. And for those I love, I'd tell them more often.

I would concentrate more on those few talents I may have to make them productive. I would try to be more content with myself even as I strive to improve.

I would try to memorize more Bible verses.

I would read the actual book instead of CliffsNotes.

I would never again make the accumulation and possession of money a major criterion for determining success. (Just because it has been a criterion doesn't mean I achieved it.)

I would seek the company of older people more often and pay more attention to their advice and the stories they tell.

On the other hand, there are probably more things I would do again than things I would change.

I would still go to church.

I would still love my family.

I would still seek out and cherish the company of friends.

That about sums up everything that's important.

Usually toward the end of my reflection, I try to draw some philosophical conclusions. After all, it would be a waste to have no useful outcome from the activity. So, I have concluded that it is a great deal better to do all the things you want to do than to spend the rest of your life wishing you had — even if you make mistakes along the way.

Heroes Still

There aren't many heroes anymore. Even those we used to think were heroes — Mickey Mantle, Babe Ruth, John Wayne, John Kennedy — are all victims of revisionist historians who seem bent on exposing the feet of clay of every human we admired.

I wish they wouldn't do that. We all know that nobody's perfect, that even those we admire have human flaws. But don't remind me of it. Let me have my fantasy. Let me see my heroes as I want them to be: bigger than life and immune from the vicissitudes that affect the rest of us.

There had to be some outstanding quality that initially endeared us to our heroes, something that set them apart from the crowd of similarly occupied people. It may have been a physical ability, or an artistic talent, or courage, or any of several other qualities. But whatever it was, they were different from you and me.

They were symbols of worthy goals. They stood on a pedestal reserved for those who were singular in their achievements, who exuded qualities of performance far beyond our mortal capacity to achieve. They gave us something to look at as we worked toward our more mundane goals.

Today's young people have a dearth of heroes from which to choose. In all honesty, we looked for heroes in the same places during our youth: the movies, stage, sports, and the military. Sometimes a hero would come along from more ordinary professions: a lifeguard who saved someone from drowning, the man who chased a robber down the street, or the law enforcement officer who caught the crooks. Now, all heroes are so scrutinized by the press that all of their personal flaws are exposed along with their heroic achievements so that the achievements, no matter how meritorious, are diminished by the exposure of imperfections.

Often this revelation is conducted by those who declare we have a "right to know" the truth about these folks. If that is the case, then I must say that, in many cases, ignorance is bliss. If a man can hit a baseball out of the park today, let me revel with him in that achievement. Don't diminish the moment because someone else has hit more or because the ball is "livelier." If he can lead men into battle by setting an example of courage, I don't want to know that he is an illegitimate child. If he can swim under the ice of a frozen lake to save a child, I don't care or want to know if he declared bankruptcy. If he can lead a nation bogged down in cynicism into a world free from war and famine, I don't want to know if he fights with his wife. Let me admire the good in every person.

I don't want to seem Pollyannaish or unrealistic. I just want to see that everything in life is not dark, that real people can have good and bad qualities, and that we can admire those good qualities without emphasizing the bad.

So despite the current trend to revise history's assessment of heroes, I still admire Mickey Mantle because each time he hit a home run I ran the bases with him. I still admire John Wayne because each time he stood up to the bad guys in the movies I was there with him when he fought them. I still admire John Kennedy for bringing a feeling of optimism to the young people of the 1960s because I was one of those young people.

All of my heroes are still my heroes.

∾ ∾ ∾

CHAPTER NINE

---

the wonderful world of fiction

∾ ∾ ∾

The Fourth of July Parade

It was hard to believe that this was the first Fourth of July parade we had ever had in Bogue. I mean, we have been in existence, the town of Bogue that is, since 1854. I don't know why nobody ever thought to have a parade sometime between then and now.

'Cept maybe during The War. By that I mean the War Between the States. You know, there were a lot of folks around here who didn't really get involved in that particular war. They figured they didn't really have a dog in that fight. Not many people around here owned slaves, and everybody was led to believe that was just part of the reason for the war. My great-granddaddy used to tell me the war was fought 'cause we didn't want nobody in Washington telling us what we could and could not do in Bogue.

That's still pretty much the case.

Now we did have some kin who stood up for The Cause, whatever it was. They went off and fought, and some of them got killed, and some of them come back home just like any other war. Everybody was proud of the ones who fought in the war, and we did put up a monument to the Confederacy right there on the courthouse lawn. But I do know for sure that somewhere along the line, it became more important to be called an American than a Rebel. Least it is for most people.

That's why I can't understand why we hadn't had a Fourth of July parade before now. We've got a Lions Club, and a Woman's Club, and a

Jaycees, and the Veterans of Foreign Wars has got a clubhouse that's the only place where you can get a semi-legal drink of liquor in this town. You'd think that somebody in that bunch would've come up with the idea of a parade before now.

Now, all this is not to say that we have never celebrated the Fourth of July. Lord, no. Why, we have the biggest Fourth of July picnic and fireworks you have ever seen. That's been going on ever since I can remember. In fact, that fireworks display gets bigger every year. Somebody said that last year there was more than two thousand head of people out to the baseball field to watch the fireworks.

The fireworks show has a special, personal connection for me. It was at the fireworks show back in '51 that I met Arabella Shaw. I was home on leave from the war in Korea, and she was visiting my sister, Louise, for the holiday. She went with me to the show, and we had a really good time. Without going into detail, I'll just say that the fireworks in the sky over the ball field couldn't compare to the fireworks under the grandstand.

Just before this parade was supposed to start, I took a folding chair and set it up right on the corner in front of my service station. I figured what with the traffic all blocked off, there wouldn't be any customers, and I might as well take advantage of the station being right on the parade route and across from the courthouse.

The parade route started out to the high school and come down Main Street and ended up at the old train depot. The courthouse sits right smack in the middle of the intersection of Main Street and Vine Street. That's why they had set up the reviewing stand on the courthouse lawn.

I heard the siren blowing even before I saw the sheriff's car leading the parade. Sheriff Hinson always led every parade, and his wife always sat beside him. She had been the Pork Festival Queen back before she got married and still loved to be in parades. He had convinced her, by threatening to lock her in the jail, not to wear her Pork Festival crown.

When they came around the courthouse, all the dignitaries in the reviewing stand applauded. They did that for every entry all through the parade. Most of the dignitaries were members of the chamber of commerce. They were the ones who come up with the idea of having the parade. Of course, the mayor and the town council and the police chief were all sitting up there, too.

Lee Callahan, the parade marshal, was right behind the sheriff's car. Lee was probably the most decorated war hero we had. He had fought in Vietnam and been wounded. He had a bunch of medals, and he was wearing them on his uniform. He looked real pleased with himself sitting there on the trunk of that restored '61 Thunderbird convertible.

The high school band was playing loud and strong as they come around the courthouse and stopped right in front of the reviewing stand to do a little concert. It was not the best performance they had ever given. Jimmy Lee Evers, the band director, had a time getting his band members to come back from their summer vacation to play in the parade. He had only about three-fourths of the group there, and some of the important parts were missing. Like the bass drum, for instance. It's real hard for a marching band to march without a bass drum and no drum major. Somebody's supposed to keep the rhythm together. Jimmy Lee was doing the best he could, but Joleen Caldwell, the chief (and only) majorette, was distracting him and everybody else what with her all about to fall out of her costume every time she dropped her baton. Which was often.

Leroy McPherson was driving the fire truck right behind the band. He didn't help matters any by continuously blowing that siren while the band was playing. Then again, that might have been the band's saving grace. They could blame the fire truck for the sound the crowd was hearing.

Miss Bogue County was right behind the fire truck. She was sitting on the trunk of a red Corvette that just matched her red, sequined evening gown. She just sparkled in the sunlight as she smiled at everybody. That blonde hair never moved. I figured she had put enough hairspray on there to keep it still in the middle of a hurricane. She had a diagonal sash that read "Miss Bogue County." She had just come back from being in the Miss North Carolina Pageant where she had won a Most Talented Non-Finalist Award for her up-tempo piano arrangement of "Moonlight Sonata." Appropriately, she will officially set off the first set of fireworks at the show tonight.

Behind Miss Bogue County was a big John Deere tractor pulling a flatbed trailer loaded with about 20 little cloggers. They had a great big boom box playing bluegrass music and they were dancing up a storm. The most amazing thing to me was how those little folks could dance like that on a moving stage. I remembered how hard it was to dance at the Strawberry Festival when I just *thought* the stage was moving. The banner on the side of the trailer said "Miss Collins Dance Academy." The older lady dancing along with the children was Miss Collins. She had gotten her start in dancing when she was in so many beauty pageants when she was younger. I don't think she ever won a title, but she was always a talent winner. She seemed to be having a great time dancing and waving to the crowd and keeping her brood concentrating on their dancing.

The VFW float was right behind the dancers. These old fellows had on their little hats that we have all come to respect and admire over the years. Everybody knows that these are the men who fought for our country in the World Wars and Korea, and there were some there who had fought in the Vietnam War. Some of them are getting kind of feeble. Some had lost a leg or an arm in the fighting. I should've been up there with them. I thought it was interesting that we had two VFW posts in the county — one black and one white — but they were both on the same parade float. They all waved and hollered at me as they went by. I thought as they passed, "We will never see their like again."

I had been so caught up in watching the parade, I didn't notice somebody had set up a folding chair and sat down beside me. When I finally noticed, I just about fell out on the sidewalk. There sitting next to me was Arabella Shaw. I didn't have a bit of trouble recognizing her after all those years. She was still as pretty as I remembered her despite a few little wrinkles around her eyes and a touch of gray in her hair.

"Hello, Henry," she said.

"Oh, my," I said. "Arabella Shaw." That's all I could say. The smell of her perfume and the smile on her face just hypnotized me. I felt like a schoolboy. I kept looking at her with my mouth open.

Finally, Arabella said, "Well, is that all you have to say after all these years? Aren't you going to tell me how pretty I still am and how I haven't aged a bit? Where is that smooth-talking soldier boy I knew?" Arabella could always flirt like a good Southern belle.

"The old soldier is right here, but he's not as smooth as he used to be, and he can't react to surprises like he used to, either. What in the world brought you back to Bogue?" I asked.

"The parade, of course. I read about it in the paper, and I guess the memory of a Fourth of July many years ago just made me nostalgic for Bogue," she replied. "When I asked some folks in town if you were still around anywhere, they told me you had a service station. So here I am."

Then we both got struck mute. I wanted to ask her a bunch of questions, but I didn't want to be too forward. She turned and seemed to be caught up in watching the Cotillion Club float.

I pointed to the young lady on the raised platform of the float and said, "You remember Inez McElroy; used to live out at ol' man Ritter's place? That's her daughter up there. She got selected to lead the cotillion this year. You know, Inez married Larry Bryan right after they graduated from high school. Larry's the only man I know to make money selling Amway. He got to be the Imperial Wizard or something like that. Took his money and invested it in the oil and gas distributorship here and got richer. Understand Inez does the best she can to keep ol' Larry from being too wealthy."

I didn't figure I needed to go into what all Inez had done. Everybody in town knew Inez had been messing around with that lawyer in Wilmington, but nobody wanted to embarrass Larry by letting on they knew anything. I figured Arabella probably knew the fellow in Wilmington, but I didn't want to bring it up. Course, gossip being what it is in this town, the lawyer might not even exist.

I looked over at Arabella kind of sideways, hoping she wouldn't see me looking. She was still a good-looking woman. Her hair was fixed real nice, and she dressed like those ladies at the bank — real conservative but expensive looking. And here I was sitting out here in my dirty overalls, a day-old growth of beard, and smelling like Quaker State.

"Preacher Smith still here?" she asked. "I came by the parsonage on the way into town and saw a blue ribbon on the lamp post. I figured somebody had a baby boy."

"Preacher Smith died about four months ago. Old age, I reckon. New preacher lives there now. Young fellow. Got six or eight children. Guess preachers got a lot of time on their hands."

Arabella laughed then, and we just sat there and talked and didn't pay much attention to the parade. We caught up on each other's lives. Both our spouses had died, and our children were all grown up and gone. We showed each other pictures of our grandchildren. She had retired from teaching school and still lived near Wilmington. She knew about the death of my sister, her friend of long ago. Our conversation was interrupted by the sound of the "ooga" horns emanating from the antique cars passing in the parade. "Remember those?" I asked.

"Oh, yes," she replied. "That one right there looks just like the one we used to ride in when we came from Wilmington to Bogue. It was still just a little two-lane road then and hardly any traffic on it. Mama used to pack a lunch, and we'd stop along the way to eat. No fast-food places for us." And she laughed a girlish laugh that had not changed in 50 years.

I recalled that "the first time I went to Wilmington was on the old Atlantic Coast Line railroad. That was real excitement for a little boy from Bogue. A big trip. Can't do that now. They took up the tracks."

"That doesn't mean you can't drive down there now. With the new highway, it's just a short trip. You could visit old friends, you know."

About that time the horses brought up the end of the parade. I always thought that was a wise move, to make the horses the last thing in a parade. It was particularly considerate of the folks marching in the band.

People started picking up their lawn chairs and walking back to their homes or to their cars. It always looked strange to me to see people walking down the middle of the street, even when I knew the street had been blocked off to traffic. I kept expecting to see somebody get hit by a car.

The thought of asking Arabella if she was going to watch the fireworks had been in the back of my mind almost from the time she put her chair down beside me, but I was almost afraid to ask. So I just kind of blurted it out. "Are you staying for the fireworks display?"

She laughed that girlish laugh and for some reason it seemed like it was 1951 again. "Well, I had thought about it, but I didn't have anybody to go with me," she said. "And I don't think I would enjoy it all by myself."

"Well, uh, I'd be glad to go with you," I offered.

"Would you, Henry?" she asked. "That would be nice."

So, I'm going with Arabella to the Fourth of July fireworks display at nine o'clock tonight. We'll watch the show this time. Then again, maybe not.

The Tent Revival

Saturday night, August 23, 1956, was the night the Holy Ghost was supposed to visit Flynn's Crossing. Least that's what the signs said that me and John Lee had been putting up all over town. The hand-lettered signs said, "*Prepare to Meet God. See the Holy Ghost at Work. 7:00 p.m. Sam Leonard's Pasture Saturday night only.*"

A long-legged preacher had give us 50 cents apiece to put the signs all over town. We had a lot more signs than there was places in Flynn's Crossing to put them, so we had put a whole bunch on one telephone pole. We had to buy our own tacks from Mr. Gallaway's hardware store anyway, and we didn't want to spend all our money so we didn't buy but a few.

The preacher had give us the signs about a week before the Holy Ghost was suppose to come to Flynn's Crossing. We had no idea how the preacher was going to get the Holy Ghost there or what was going to happen when He got there. But 50 cents was 50 cents, you know what I mean.

Anyhow, come Saturday morning about 10 o'clock the preacher showed up with a truck that had "*Prepare to Meet God. Glorious Day Ministry Revivals*" wrote on the side. We saw him come into town so we followed him on our bicycles out to Mr. Leonard's place. He drove right out into the middle of a hay field that had just been cut and baled earlier that week. I always liked the smell of a new-cut hay field, and the sun was baking it good that morning. Me and John Lee stopped a little ways from where the truck stopped and watched the preacher roll up the back of the truck and start unloading stuff right away.

He was a kind of tall, thin man. He had on a pair of khaki pants and a long-sleeved white shirt with the sleeves rolled up. His hair was slicked down with enough hair cream, probably Wildroot Cream Oil, to have slid a pig through a keyhole.

He had unrolled what looked like a big tarpaulin when a woman come driving up in a brand-new Cadillac. Now, I tell you what, that woman was dressed up. We hadn't ever seen anybody dressed that fancy except in the movies. When she got out of that car, I declare I thought she looked just like Ava Gardner. And since me and John Lee liked to look at Ava Gardner, we looked real hard at this lady.

She went over to where the preacher was unloading stuff and started talking to him. We couldn't hear what they were saying, but whatever it was didn't take too long because in a few minutes she got back in that Cadillac and drove outta that pasture like the law was after her.

About that time the preacher saw me and John Lee and waved for us to come over to where he was. When we did he said he'd give us a quarter to go find Mr. Leonard and the people that was supposed to help him set up his tent. That's when we learned what he was doing there. He said he was going to have a tent revival right there in Mr. Leonard's pasture.

Didn't me or John Lee know exactly what a tent revival was, but we figured we'd go find Mr. Leonard and he'd tell us. We didn't want to appear ignorant in front of the preacher, so we did what he asked without any questions. A quarter is a quarter, you know what I mean.

We run over to Mr. Leonard's store and told him what the preacher wanted. He told some fellas that were sitting around the store to go on over and help the preacher. After they left I asked Mr. Leonard what all a tent revival was.

He said, "It's about the same as Sunday morning preachin' except it's held under a tent. There's lots of singin' and preachin' and it's a time when sinners can repent and keep from goin' to Hell."

"Is that when they meet the Holy Ghost?" asked John Lee.

"Yeah, I guess you could say that. Why don't you boys come on over tonight and see for yourself? If you want to, you can sit with me and Mrs. Leonard. We'd be glad to have you," he offered.

We thanked him for the invitation, told him we might be there, bought two Co' Colas and a can of Viennas and left the store.

That afternoon we watched the men unload the truck and set up the tent. We began to speculate about this revival. Both of us went to the Methodist church there in Flynn's Crossing every Sunday. But to tell you the truth, we didn't always pay attention like we ought to, and there was a lot of blank spaces when it come to religious stuff. After all, there's just so much you can understand when you're only 11 years old, you know what I mean.

At supper that night I told Mama that me and John Lee was going to the revival with Mr. Leonard and his wife. She said she was surprised that the Leonards was going. Methodists didn't usually care for the kind of "carrying on" that took place at tent revivals. I didn't exactly know what she meant by "carrying on," but if Mama was against it, I sure wanted to know what it was. She didn't say I couldn't go, so I got on my bicycle and met John Lee at the road going into the hay field.

It was a hot August night, so it surprised me to see the men show up wearing coats and ties. The women had on their Sunday dresses, and a lot of them wore hats. Mr. Leonard had on a suit, and Mrs. Leonard was dressed real nice. She didn't wear a hat, but she had her hair tied up in a tight bun with a big hatpin run through it.

While we were sitting with the Leonards toward the back of the tent, I noticed that more and more of the people weren't dressed up. Some of the men coming in had on bib overalls with white shirts and the collars buttoned all the way up. I knew most of these folks, and you could tell they were mostly farmers 'cause the faces were tanned, but the top part of their foreheads was white from wearing hats in the field. These folks sat toward the front of the tent.

There wasn't much breeze blowing, but the sides of the tent had been rolled up, and every once in a while the air would stir a little bit. There was a kinda mixture of smells, all kinds of perfume and a good dose of Old Spice after-shave. I did recognize just a hint of Evening in Paris perfume because that was the kind my Aunt Minnie, Daddy's sister, wore to the Sunday school picnic and near 'bout every other time she left the house. When I smelled that perfume I looked for Aunt Minnie, but I never did see her. Mama told me later that Aunt Minnie had about quit going out since she had give up on ever finding a husband.

As the people would come in, the men would all shake hands and the women would hug each other. The men talked to the men, and the women talked to the women, neither one letting on that the other sex was even there.

After a while the lady we had seen driving the Cadillac came in and went up on the stage and began to play the piano. She didn't have a hymnbook, but she played pretty lively and didn't stop between songs.

Then the preacher came out and said a few words and prayed. Then the two of 'em, the preacher and the piano player, began to sing together. As I listened to them sing, I was reminded of what Miss Irene Sadler, the music teacher at school, had told us. She said most times when people can't sing too good they sing loud.

After they had sung a couple of songs together, the preacher walked over to the middle of the stage and began his sermon. He told everybody that before they left that night they would see a miracle. While the two had been singing, I had thought maybe me and John Lee would leave early, but after he promised a miracle, I decided we'd go ahead and stick around.

That preacher had an unusual way of speaking once he started his sermon. He was talking real loud and about every other word he would kinda grunt and take a big breath. I could tell he was really getting excited about what he was saying. Sometimes he would say the same thing over and over. I figured he was doing that to stall for time until he could think of something else to say.

The more he talked the more he'd sweat. He took off his coat and threw it over toward the piano player. She picked it up and placed it on the top of the piano. The rest of the folks must have been just as excited 'cause the other men started taking off their coats, and you could see how wet their shirts were.

As best I could tell, he was telling us all that we were going to Hell if we didn't change. He said God was going to strike us all if we didn't straighten up and fly right. The preacher said he was a lot like Abraham when God said he was going to destroy Sodom and Gomorrah. He said he was looking for 10 righteous people, but hadn't found any in Flynn's Crossing. I didn't know how he had been able to make that determination since he had just got to town and didn't know hardly anybody.

He went on to tell about Lot and his family and how they had run out of town before God cleaned it out and how his wife had turned to salt. He said we all needed to confess our sins, no matter how bad they were. That's when he told everybody who had sinned to come up to the stage and tell him all about it, and they would be cleaned and could go on to heaven.

I didn't know there was so many sinful people in Flynn's Crossing, but just about everybody there got up and started walking to the preacher. The lady started playing the piano again, but a lot more mournful than she had played at the beginning. They all were crying and the preacher was hugging them and blessing them.

About the time I figured they had quit confessing their sins, the preacher said it was time for all those who had some kind of affliction to come forward and be healed. He said this was the time for miracles.

Well, this is what me and John Lee had been waiting for. I was looking for some kind of bright, white light to come shining down like I had seen in the movies, and a choir to start singing, and the Holy Spirit would glide down and land on the stage.

That didn't happen. What did happen wasn't even close to what I expected. Mr. Watson Clark went up there and told the preacher he had water on his knee and it made it painful for him to walk. The preacher kneeled down on that stage right in front of Mr. Clark and grabbed the old man's knee and shook it. I thought Mr. Clark was going to fall down right there, but he didn't. He just stood there until the preacher told him to walk. And he did walk, but I couldn't tell that he walked any different than he had before, but everybody started shouting and Mr. Clark was crying.

Miss Corina Ellsworth said she had terrible headaches, so the preacher clapped both hands on top of her head and prayed. He shook her head so hard, her steel-rimmed glasses come off. She didn't even pick them up, just lifted her arms and said she was pain-free and walked off the stage.

Mr. Lacy Conway brought his daughter, Louise, up to the preacher and told him that Louise was suffering from a heart murmur. Louise was a good-sized girl who weighed a good 250 pounds. My grandma had said that Louise hadn't seen her feet since she got out of high school. Without any hesitation, the preacher reached out and placed his hands on both sides of Louise's chest and squeezed as hard as he could and began to pray. Evidently, Louise's heart murmur didn't keep her from knocking that preacher upside the head so hard he fell flat on his back stretched out on the stage. Louise walked off all puffed up with her daddy right behind her.

The piano player quit playing and went over to the preacher. She picked up his head and got him to open his eyes, then she slapped him so hard he went back out again.

Mrs. Leonard said all that was outrageous and took Mr. Leonard by the hand and told me and John Lee to come on with her. We went on outside, and the Leonards got in their car and drove off. Me and John Lee headed for our bicycles, but we didn't leave right away.

We stayed around and watched the rest of the people leave. When they were all gone, we saw the preacher talking to the piano player; then, she went and got in her Cadillac and drove off, too.

The next morning on the way to church we had to drive right by the tent. It was still up, but the preacher's truck was gone and so was the preacher. That tent stayed up for about a week until Mr. Leonard sent some of his crew over there to take it down. They rolled it up and put it in the back of Mr. Leonard's fertilizer warehouse. They divided up the chairs among the churches and the volunteer fire department and took the piano to the schoolhouse. The preacher never came back to claim it.

It was almost a year later that the preacher at the Methodist church preached about the situation at Sodom and Gomorrah. He made some good points, but somehow the service didn't have the same excitement as it did out at the tent revival, you know what I mean?

Oh, to Be Miss Beauville

When the Jaycee fellow came to my house and asked me to be in the Miss Beauville Pageant, I thought he was crazy. I had never thought of myself as pretty, and nobody other than my mama and daddy ever told me I was. But there he was, sitting in my living room just as proper as you please, talking about the scholarship money I could win if I was to be Miss Beauville.

I had seen the girls at school who had won beauty titles and the thought never crossed my mind that I would even come close to being like them. Even on their worst days, they always had their hair looking just right and even wore lipstick to gym class.

Most of the cheerleading squad held some kind of title. Jimmi Sue Thornton was the Tomato Queen for the whole state. She had a crown with a lot of rhinestones in it, and right in the middle of the thing was this big, tomato-shaped group of red rhinestones. It was pretty impressive.

Most of the other girls were queens for some festival or other. Seemed like folks around here celebrate every fresh fruit and vegetable and most of the livestock. There was a Collard Queen and a Watermelon Queen and a Peach Queen and there was even one girl who was a Spot Queen. A spot is a fish, you know.

But this Jaycee fellow was talking about Miss Beauville, which is a preliminary to the Miss North Carolina Pageant. That means that whoever wins the Miss Beauville title goes on to the Miss North Carolina Pageant in Raleigh, and if she wins then she can go on to Miss America right up there in Atlantic City. Well, when he told me that, I knew right then he was being too ambitious for this girl.

But I should have known that my daddy could match anybody when it came to being proud of his daughter. He has been known to take my report card to church and show it to the members of his Sunday school class. And when my little brother nominated me for Tar Heel Youth Baseball Queen, my daddy gave the team $100 cash. That's how the winner was selected. Whoever raised the most money for the team got the title.

So when this Jaycee said that I was pretty and talented and smart, my daddy more than agreed with him. When he kept telling Daddy about the scholarship money, he pretty much settled the situation. So we filled out the application form. I was going to be in the pageant.

That visit was on Sunday afternoon, and I was supposed to go to a preliminary meeting of all the contestants the next Saturday morning. During the week I mentioned to some of my friends that I was going to be in the pageant and asked them what they thought about it. I really didn't have to ask. They would have told me anyway. Especially Penny Ivey. Penny was the most opinionated girl I ever knew and was always more than willing to let you know what her opinion was.

"Cora Thurman," she said, "you got no business being in a pageant. All those pageant girls are so stuck up they're liable to drown in a heavy rain. You're not like them. Some of those girls do this pageant thing like it was a matter of life or death. They have been in literally hundreds of pageants since they were big enough to toddle across a stage."

I told her it wasn't really my decision, that Daddy had made up his mind and I was just doing what he wanted. Besides, what did I have to lose?

"Your dignity," was Penny's response. "Do you realize that you have got to walk around on that stage wearing a bathing suit and high heel shoes? Now, how dignified is that?"

If I had been thinking at the time, I would have probably decided right then not to be in the pageant. I had just got used to looking at my body in the mirror without being embarrassed. I did not have what they called "a balanced body." That meant I was not proportioned like the models in the mail-order catalogs. Part of me hung over where there shouldn't have been any hang-over, and other parts that should have hung didn't hang at all.

But Mama had always told me that once you make a commitment to somebody, you have to stick with it. So, bathing suit or not, I had to be in the pageant.

At the meeting on Saturday morning the real shocker hit me. The talent portion of the competition was to count more than anything else. I had planned on getting Miss Eloise, our church pianist, to accompany me while I sang "Oh, What a Beautiful Morning." That's from *Oklahoma*, you know, and it's Mama's favorite Broadway song.

But the other girls were far more prepared than I was. Some of them had gotten special taped accompaniment for their performances. They had full orchestral accompaniment for operatic songs, and one girl had an absolutely beautiful arrangement of "You Light Up My Life." It would bring tears to your eyes.

When I heard them sing their songs and saw the dancers perform their routines and that girl that twirled three batons at one time, I knew I was in over my head. This was the big time, or at least as big as it got in Beauville.

I went home and told Mama about it all and just cried. It wasn't that I was ashamed to be in the pageant. I didn't really care if I won or not. But I didn't want to disappoint Mama and Daddy.

So Mama and I talked a while and she told me some of the same things she had said so many times before. "You've got nothing to be ashamed of, Cora Mae. (She's the only one who ever called me that.) You are just as pretty as any of those girls and just as talented. Those judges aren't going to be judging their musical accompaniment. And you know as well as I do that most of what's in those girls' bathing suits is not them at all. So let's just go ahead and you do the best you can, which is all God or anybody else requires, and we'll not even say anything to your daddy about this. He's already told his Sunday school class."

Penny went with me and Mama to look for a gown for the evening gown competition.

We went to Belk's and to The Bridal Nook; then we finally wound up at Miss Cornelia's Center for Pageant Design. Miss Cornelia used to sew for just about everybody in town until she made a gown one time for the girl who won Miss Sweet Potato. After that, she had so many requests for gowns she became a pageant specialist. I had told Mama I didn't see any need in us putting a lot of money into an expensive gown that I probably wouldn't ever wear again, but Penny said if I was going to be in this thing, I should do it right. We talked to Miss Cornelia about a black gown with a bunch of beaded stuff on it. She had one at her house that she had made for a girl who was going to be in the Miss Flame Pageant that the fire station was having. But they canceled the pageant after the fire station burned down, and Miss Cornelia was stuck with the gown.

That gown must have weighed close to 50 pounds. When I tried it on, I knew I would look funny trying to walk down the runway in that thing. Just trying to look poised and graceful without breaking a sweat in that heavy gown would probably qualify me for some kind of prize.

After a while even Penny agreed that it didn't make any sense to spend a lot of money on a "competition" gown. Mama went back to the house and found the gown I had worn to the prom when Leon McCormick took me back in the spring. In his usual understated way, Leon had told me I looked "fit to be with" that night. I guess if I could get Leon to say that much, that gown would do for about any pageant.

For the next couple of months I had a regular routine. I'd go to school, come home, do my homework, go over to Miss Eloise's and practice my song, then come back home and lift sandbags. Daddy had figured that lifting sandbags would build up my "upper body," meaning my bust. Mama had told him that was one of my concerns. Every week he'd add some more sand to the bags. I never could see much improvement. Finally, Penny and I went down to Belk's and bought some foam rubber pads to fit inside the top of my bathing suit. Daddy thought the sandbags worked wonders.

Mrs. Whittingham, the pageant director, told us to read up on all the current events and be able to talk about all the attributes of Beauville as training for the interview portion of the pageant competition. She said it didn't really matter what we answered to the judges as long as it was spoken well. That didn't make a lot of sense to me, but I found out I should never question Mrs. Whittingham. She had been in pageants herself many years ago and was always telling us how she had won her titles. The fact that she had been a beauty queen at some time in the dim, dark past did not make my winning a similar title a very worthwhile quest.

Anyway, I persevered through the remaining weeks of the pageant training, and when the day of the pageant finally came I was ready to get on with it.

The interviews were held that afternoon at the country club. I had never been there and was impressed with the size of the place. The room where we contestants waited our turn to go in for the interview was really pretty, but I felt like I shouldn't sit down on the furniture. That was a good idea anyway since I didn't want to wrinkle the new suit Mama and I had picked out. It was pink, and I wore a white silk blouse with a single strand of Mama's pearls. Daddy said pearls always showed good taste and let everybody know you were a lady.

The interviews were timed to last just five minutes. Five people, two men and three women, sat behind a table, and I sat in a chair placed far enough back that they could see my new dyed-to-match pumps.

They were all really nice folks who mostly asked me questions about things I had written on my application. They also asked what was my favorite color and if I could be anybody else in the world who would I be. I told them I wouldn't want to be anybody else, but if I had to choose I'd like to be Sandra O'Connor, the Supreme Court judge. Penny and I had guessed they would ask that question, and Penny said I should tell them I wanted to be a Supreme Court judge because I looked good in black. Penny was kind of shallow sometimes. I actually told them I admired her because she had shown that women could reach heights once only held by men. They seemed to like that.

That night at the pageant I was really relaxed. I knew I wasn't going to win, so I just decided to let the other girls get all nervous. We got through all the phases of competition without much incident. The girl did drop her baton once, but she said it was because she was used to twirling it when both ends were on fire and they wouldn't let her have fire in the auditorium. A baton twirler had about burned the place down during a pageant a few years ago.

When we got to the evening gown competition, I walked out in that white gown with the sequins around the waist that I had worn to the prom. I thought it looked pretty good, and when I caught a look at Daddy when I walked down the ramp I could see a tear in his eye even if he was grinning from ear to ear.

Finally, the emcee called everybody back out to announce the winners. We all held hands and looked anxious. He first announced the winner of the Miss Congeniality Award. When he said my name, I about died. Penny told me later on that she knew then I wasn't going to win because winning Miss Congeniality was a death knell for pageant winners.

There were 10 girls, and they were going to announce five places. The girl with the baton got fifth place. When they called out her name, she just nodded and stepped forward to accept her trophy. Then fourth place was the Harrelson girl, who had her hair all pulled up high on her head and tied in a knot. She smiled and curtsied when she got her trophy. Third place went to the girl who sang "You Light Up My Life." The second place, or "runnerup," was Mary Sue Horton. She was bound to have won the swimsuit competition. I told Mama that if that girl had fallen in the ocean she would never drown because there was enough foam rubber in that bathing suit to keep her afloat.

Carol McLean was the winner. When they announced her name, her hands flew to her face and she just cried like her mama had died. I was glad it was over and I hugged her just like everybody else.

Mama and Daddy took me home after the pageant reception, and we talked about the pageant on the way. Daddy was kind of quiet and kept saying how well he thought I'd done and how proud he was of me. Mama didn't say much, just smiled.

After we had a glass of milk and a piece of Mama's coconut pie, I went up to my room to go to bed. I was glad it was over. I could get on with the other things I was interested in. The only thing that bothered me was that Daddy was disappointed. He wasn't going to be able to tell his Sunday school class that his little girl was Miss Beauville.

As I turned back the covers of my bed, I saw a piece of paper on the pillow. On it, in a rough handwriting, was a single sentence that said, "All beauty comes from beautiful blood and a beautiful brain." I heard a knock on my door, and Daddy came in. He said, "That's the only thing I remember Miss Bailey teaching me in high school English. Mr. Walt Whitman must have known my little girl." And he closed the door.

About the Author

Born and raised in Hallsboro, Bill Thompson graduated from Campbell College (now Campbell University) with a degree in English. Having lived most of his life in southeastern North Carolina, he has worked as a teacher, a morning television-show host, and an entertainer. He has served as master of ceremonies for countless festivals, celebrations, and beauty contests and is a popular speaker for conventions throughout the state.

Most of Bill's professional career, however, has been spent furthering the cause of the Boys and Girls Homes of North Carolina, a statewide, nonprofit organization that provides year-round residential care for children ages 10 to 18 at Lake Waccamaw. Having first come to work for the organization in 1966, Bill was elected president in February 2003. Prior to this appointment, he served as vice president for institutional advancement.

Bill's no stranger to the printed page. For more than 20 years, the Columbus County native has amused readers of various newspapers in the Carolinas with tales, observations, and reflections of what he loves and knows best — life in North Carolina. Since 2001, he has delighted readers of *Our State* magazine with his warm, folksy column "Front Porch Stories." (Bill also hosts a television show called "Front Porch Stories.")

In this collection of essays, Bill further explores his down-home roots and the people who shaped him into the character he is today. *Sweet Tea, Fried Chicken, and Lazy Dogs: Reflections on North Carolina Life* comprises 56 essays that touch on his observations and treasured memories, including such topics as food, farming, animals, music, family, and neighbors. These lighthearted and insightful commentaries and short stories celebrate the essence of rural and small-town life in North Carolina.

Bill and his wife, Linda, make their home in Hallsboro. His daughter, Mari, lives in Charlotte. His son, Will, resides in Whiteville, just a few miles from Hallsboro. When he's not on the road or writing, Bill enjoys riding horses, singing in the church choir, and savoring his daily afternoon snack — a Pepsi and a pack of Nabs.